CW00404566

How to
write for
magazines
...in one weekend

by Diana Cambridge

CANAL STREET PUBLISHING

NB also:
Linda JONES : The Greatest freelance
writing Tips in the world (2008)

Published by Canal Street Publishing Ltd.
1 Coburg Villas, Camden Road, Bath, Somerset, BA1 5JF.
www.canalstreet.org.uk
First published in Great Britain in 2006.

Designer: Richard Gale

A catalogue record for this book is available from The British Library.

ISBN 10: 0-9553391-0-3
ISBN 13: 978-0-9553391-0-3

Printed and bound by HSW Print
Tel. 01443 441100

How to write for magazines ...in one weekend

Contents

Hello,

You're a writer and you'd love to see your work published in magazines – and get paid for it. But residential writing courses can be expensive and time consuming, sticking with evening classes is tough and many how-to books are instantly forgettable. When you sit down to write, you may be overcome by inertia, worry or lack of confidence, which can also hold you back from submitting work you've finished.

In my experience, it's not rejection that stops talented writers seeing their work in print, it's the fact that they never get to send their work to editors. They're stopped in their tracks by a confidence crisis.

Like most writers, I need quick results to shore up my confidence. Even after a lifetime spent successfully in journalism, both newspapers and magazines, I still have times when nothing happens, when I need inspiration and something to get me started. The weekend is an ideal time, yet I've wasted many staring at my computer, starting and stopping different writing projects, and gazing out of the window.

If I'd had a coach to tell me what and how to write at these times, and an inspiring and practical timetable to follow, I would have achieved so much more. I know friends and readers who suffer in the same way.

My solution is a relaxing but structured writing programme you can do in a weekend. But the weekend won't be all slog. I want you to enjoy it and to treat it as a refreshing change, which will also lead you to new skills – and to profit. Whether you want to write a reader's letter to a magazine, a travel article, an opinion piece on parenting or work, or an article on your own city – I give you practical insider advice for all these and more.

Starting from Friday evening, you'll be indulging that part of you which knows you can write – and you'll be switching off from the world of work and its stresses and frustrations. If you can isolate yourself for the weekend that's good, but if you have a partner or family, explain tactfully that they'll have to do without you for 48 hours. You need free time to really focus not only on your writing but also on yourself.

With my careful plan, at the end of the weekend you'll have completed work you can post off, together with the crucial marketing shot. You'll be able to choose which course options you want for the weekend, but I'd like you to try three things – a reader's letter, an opinion piece and a feature targeted at a magazine – it might be about travel, your work, your hobby, your family or a personal experience.

At the end of the 48 hours, you'll know something about the history of magazines and the way they are produced. You'll understand how it is that editorial features and paid-for advertising can co-exist in the same package. You'll have picked up the technical and journalistic skills for getting ideas, for writing and structuring articles, for marketing your work, and for keeping going.

It won't be painful or tiring. I show you, step by step, just what to do. I even have ideas for interesting foods and drinks to sustain you and give you energy for these two days. I encourage you all the way. And you can take this programme at any time, if your break from your job falls in the middle of the week.

Even best-selling authors use writing coaches!

Let me be yours over this weekend.

Diana

1 – Take that first step

'There is no secret of success in writing except individuality, or call it personality.'
~ Patricia Highsmith

It's Friday and you've chosen this weekend for your at-home writing course. This will be a truly great 48 hours for you. Welcome to one of your most enjoyable, productive and profitable weekends!

Think of this weekend as a luxury magazine writing course, customised for you… with achievements guaranteed. You'll be spending the weekend with your personal writing coach guiding you through an enjoyable timetable. There's no hotel or conference centre to drive to, no daunting workshops to sit through, no need to read your work aloud, and you can sleep in your own comfortable bed!

By Sunday evening you will have the satisfying feeling of seeing a small body of polished work piled on your desk, ready to send out to magazines – plus you'll have gained superb tools for future writing projects. You'll have picked up in one weekend what a staff magazine junior might take a year to learn.

And the market for your work is there; every magazine needs writers. You don't have to be a professional with years of journalism training and experience behind you. Often, it's the gifted amateur working as a freelance who does better in magazines. Their style is natural and fresh, and their personality shines through – they haven't become jaded with working full-time in pressured offices, churning out features to order.

Plus, if you're willing and prepared to write candidly about your own feelings and experiences, you offer a lot more value to the editor, no matter what type of magazine you are writing for. So this weekend, you'll be writing articles that come from your own thoughts and life… from you!

Capture your confidence

Confidence boosting will be a major part of your weekend course. In my experience, even gifted writers can lack the nerve to send their work out to magazines. They fear rejection – they fear their work isn't good enough. This fear can handicap them from even finishing an article. And sometimes, even from beginning it.

I've felt it myself, or I used to. Anxiety can prevent us from getting words down on paper. It can disable us. With no one there in the room at all, even completely alone at your desk, you can still feel self-conscious. Not good enough. Inadequate.

You begin to ask yourself – what's the point in even starting? Isn't it hopeless? We can easily talk ourselves into a 'why bother?' state. From there it's just a short step to opening a novel, pouring a glass of wine, switching on TV, or other sofa-related activities! All of which stop you from getting anywhere near your goal – writing.

Lack of confidence can easily sabotage your best efforts even when you've started an article. The number of writers who talk to me about their excellent ideas, even read me bits of the wonderful pieces they've written (because they've only ever written bits), listen to my sincere praise, and then never finish what they started, always makes me sad.

With many writers, even as I am applauding their work, I can sense their disbelief. Some even ask me to repeat my praise in different ways, several times, as though they have not heard it! They may even suggest that I don't mean it; that I'm making it up just to please them. Some actually accuse me of 'just being nice'.

But that would be pointless. I am not reluctant to offer constructive criticism. I've also been known to nag my staff writers at work. 'Just being nice' for the sake of it isn't one of my charms. Some writers appear to think I'm pretending their ideas are good, their writing fine. Some even look for ways to find flaws in work I've just told them was great.

'You say it's fine? Well, what about that paragraph on page two… I don't feel I've done it very well… I'm not very happy with it… it's OK, but not really that good, is it?'

Free your talent

Even when they've finished a piece, it's rare for a young writer to take my advice to send a piece to a national magazine – where they would have great success. They're reluctant to develop ideas and do extra work to move their career on. What a valuable investment that might be. Yet hardly any of them are prepared to spend the time, or have the confidence (and motivation and confidence go hand- in-hand), to do it. But for the few – like you – who will, what rewards you'll scoop!

Yes, I've had protégés who have won writing competitions. They went on to get their work published nationally and achieve good jobs in publishing – all because they were prepared to go a little further, to put in a bit more, work even harder, even when there were setbacks.

What sets successful writers apart is that rejections don't put them off, they believe in themselves – and above all they finish work and they submit it, no matter what. Equally talented writers I have known became cast down by their inability to finish articles, lost faith in themselves, and gave up.

Does anything I've said ring true for you and your lack of writing confidence? It maybe that this defeatist attitude was ingrained in you by parents who constantly criticized, or by school teachers who put you down. It might very easily be a bullying boss at work who has dented your self-esteem.

But that doesn't matter now; ignore them, and move on!

You can, with practice, train yourself to be more confident as a writer. You keep reinforcing your talent in your mind, your willingness to learn, your desire to succeed. Keep that happy image of you, the successful writer, in your mind.

I will be at your side over the next two days, helping you all the way. Allow this weekend to release your inner confidence, let your creativity shine through – and even get you and your completed work to the postbox!

What can you achieve in one weekend?

Quite a lot. You can choose from two or three short reader's letters, or one short article destined for a weekly magazine, plus one personal piece for a women's magazine, or one local piece for a city or county magazine.

I'd like you to try one travel piece – based on any location and any journey in the UK or abroad. But if you don't want to try the travel option, you could write a short piece based on your work or family, or a topic such as food, money, or a hobby.

That's at least three pieces of varying length which you can send off on Monday morning – or even Sunday evening if you feel like it. You can pick your options from the course. Then make your list of choices, which might be:

2 reader's letters
1 travel piece
1 short opinion piece

or

Reader's handy tips for women's magazines
1 reader's letter
1 article for a woman's magazine

or

1 piece for a city magazine
1 opinion piece
1 reader's letter

or

1 food piece
1 travel piece
2 reader's letters

or

any permutation of these!

Working weekend

Think the week-end's not long enough? Think again! Even with a lie-in, you could be having breakfast at around 9.30a.m, showered, dressed and at your computer with a cup of coffee at 10a.m. Let's aim for that.

You might like to work until 4p.m. with an hour's break for lunch, the ingredients for which you've already bought. That gives you five hours. If you want to start earlier or go on longer, of course that's fine – but make sure you do have some food and stretch your legs a bit.

Your weekend will be stimulating, energising and satisfying. All you have to do is prepare, plan and produce. You don't have to be perfect! And don't try to achieve too much – two or three pieces is fine.

Weekend shop

Clear your diary for Saturday and Sunday. These two days have to be your time. If you can be alone, that's just about perfect. Maybe you're even on your own at the moment with no partner in tow – look on this as an unprecedented opportunity for real me-time! If you do have a partner or family, make it plain you'll be busy most of the weekend, and that you don't want to be disturbed.

Before the weekend begins, there's a little shopping to be done. Get in everything you need; you don't need to be popping out to the 8-till-late for forgotten necessities. Besides the essentials, pamper yourself a little. Make your writing space pleasant, even a little luxurious – a few flowers might be nice.

You'll need to begin on Friday (or you could do this on Thursday) going through the list of equipment and materials for the weekend. Some of them you'll already have. Try to include them all – the cost will be far less than you'd pay for a writing weekend in a hotel or course centre – and you can choose exactly what you want to buy.

The more you prepare for your weekend, the more you'll gain from it. It will help if on Thursday you tidy your writing space a bit – no writer can work in chaos. An empty waste bin lined with fresh white paper, a stack of white copy paper, a clear desk or table, pens and pencils in a jar, a pristine note-book – these are essentials. Neatly laid out, how inspiring they look…

Here's what you'll need to buy:

▶ The magazines you're aiming to be published in – could be anything from *The Lady* to *Woman and Home* or *She*, or *Eve* to *Saga* or *Mslexia* – or a niche publication such as a travel magazine. WH Smith and the big super-market chains have loads of them, and they all need freelance writers.

▶ *Rough Guide* or *Lonely Planet* country guides if you do want to include a travel article – you'll need the country guide to your chosen destination.

▶ Local daily and weekly newspapers if you're writing a local magazine article.

▶ City or county magazine for your own area if you want to be in one.

▶ A notebook and pens.

▶ A fat, spiral-bound notebook for your personal 'coaching diary'.

▶ Spare printer cartridge.

▶ White copy paper.

▶ Paper clips.

▶ Large – A4 – envelopes, and plenty of first-class stamps.

▶ Writing magazines, which might give you ideas for extra markets. I rec-ommend *Writing*, *Writers' News* and *Mslexia*, a fine writing magazine for women, but it's a subscription-only title.

▶ Passport-size, smiling portrait pictures – 'mugshots' – of you. Get these done at a cheap booth. If you think you look good this minute, today's the day to pop into a Photo-Me-type booth! They're often at railway stations and supermarkets. Have at least a dozen copies printed. You should be smiling, not serious. Or, if you have a favourite picture, get that copied. Postcard-size is fine, too.

Indulge yourself

You must have treats on this weekend! Here's my list:

▶ One or two new paperbacks, or second hand paperbacks, you know you'll enjoy – but they're a treat for when you've finished the course.

▶ New CD, if you like music while you work – music without words is best.

▶ Flowers.

▶ Scented candles, if you like them. I've found that Morrison's super-market sell the cheapest, and their fragrance is just as pleasing as the expensive ones.

▶ A relaxing or inspirational CD, maybe to help you sleep. *Nine Ways to Touch the Soul* (www.momtazi.com) includes the soothing sound of the sea, and is designed to help writers free their creativity.

▶ An uplifting bath or shower gel to get you going in the morning – I recommend Neal's Yard Orange and Geranium Bath Oil. *(£9, Neal's Yard Remedies, www.nealsyardremedies.com)*

Soul food

You can't possibly do a writing course without delicious food and drinks to look forward to. But you don't want to spend too much time preparing and cooking. You want to use most of your time on your course, but you need to know that you have a supply of interesting and tasty food to keep you going.

You want easy meals, snacks and drinks that provide something delicious that will sustain you but not distract you from your work. If a chunk of the weekend would be taken up with a grocery shop, could you have it delivered? Sainsbury's, Tesco, and Waitrose all deliver, and some of them don't make a delivery charge. Buy all the foods you'll need for the weekend. Buy things you like and make it easy but nutritious.

Drinks? Stock up on mineral water: it's good to keep a bottle and glass on your desk. Smoothies are good for maintaining energy – you can keep going for longer and they contain a good helping of the five fruits and veg we need, though they can be high in sugar.

If you're prone to headaches, an American health fanatic I know recommends Dr Pepper canned drink. A kind of cherry cola, it's very effective for warding off headaches. But don't get hooked on it! You might find a glass or two of mineral water would also do the trick.

If you're feeling tired, drinking several glasses of mineral water can re-invigorate you. The water rehydrates your system and perks up your metabolism and concentration quickly.

Cup after cup of coffee isn't a good idea. I'd recommend one large cup of good coffee, maybe organic, when you get up and when you start the course, then stick to non-coffee drinks after that.

Wine? One glass in the evening with dinner – but only one. Any more and you'll feel groggy the next day. If you associate wine with total relaxation, and can't stop at one – best to go on the wagon for the weekend and stay with mineral water or juices. Some writers like to work with a glass of wine at their elbow. I don't really recommend it, but I confess I've succumbed once or twice. Nobody's perfect!

Yoghurt boosters

Yoghurt's an easy and highly nutritious food to include in snacks over this weekend. But if you want to make something in advance, Total Yoghurt's chef Paul Wharrier has created these energising weekend mini-meals for one. Do them all ahead – then they're ready for the breaks between course sessions.

Blue Smoothie
Mid morning Boost – Serves 1

Ingredients
150g Total 0% Greek Yoghurt
150ml Orange and Passion Fruit low calorie juice
½ a banana
25g Blueberries

Method
Blend all ingredients together in a food processor.

Garlic Yoghurt and Feta Paté
Just for Lunch – Serves 1

Ingredients
½ a clove of garlic
2 anchovy fillets
200g Total Feta Cheese
75g Total 0% Greek Yoghurt
½ tsp fresh chives, chopped
Dash of Tabasco Sauce
Ground black pepper to taste
110g butter, melted

Method
Combine the garlic, anchovies, feta, yoghurt, chives, pepper and
Tabasco sauce in a blender to a smooth paste.
Add melted butter to cheese paste and blend until smooth.
Place the mixture into a ramekin dish and set in fridge.
Turn out and serve with warm toast fingers or crusty bread and green salad.

Chilled Mango and Roasted Almonds with Total Greek Yoghurt

Sweet treat when you finish! – Serves: 1

Ingredients
75g Total 0% Greek Yoghurt
1 mango
25g whole almonds
25g honey

Method
Peel the mango using a knife or peeler, then remove the flesh from the stone.
Chill in the fridge.
Gently brown the almonds in a pan with the honey.
To serve, dice the mango into a bowl, spoon over Total Greek Yoghurt,
drizzle honey over and sprinkle almonds on top.

The office with energy

I'd like you to check two things in the space where you are working – light and air. You need both if you are to avoid that mid-afternoon slump that can set in on any weekend course. You'll be spending quite a lot of time in your room and at your computer, so you don't want it to be stuffy and draining.

I suffer from mid-afternoon slump and I tend to hunch over the computer for far too long – not something I want you to endure over your precious weekend. My friend, favourite GP and Brighton health guru, Dr Milind Jani (www. pavilionhealth.co.uk 01273 77748), says that there has to be a free circulation of air to give you a steady supply of oxygen to the brain, and to remove toxins from the office atmosphere. So, open windows. And he emphasizes the importance of taking breaks. Every hour or so is best. Unless you take breaks, your adrenaline and serotonin levels drop and they don't revive.

To up your energy and enthusiasm, move around and leave your desk once in a while. My trick is to open a window wide and then put on some favourite, tried and tested music (I like OJay's *Love Train* or The Rolling Stones *Let's Spend the Night Together*) and dance around to it. Luckily, no one sees me – and my energy does go up

Dr Jani also says that light is essential for mood elevation. Natural light is the best. A strong desk lamp is better than an overhead light. I sometimes have two, to give two pools of light on my desk.

> ### *Top tip*
>
> When writing, you can re-energise your system with a glass of ice-cold tap water. A slice of lemon or lime helps.

This is your checklist to make your weekend course run smoothly:

▶ A tidy desk and room.

▶ Keep energy food and drinks on hand.

▶ Have office scissors, paperclips, a punch and red and blue Biros.

▶ Make sure you have back-up stocks of CDs or floppy disks, and ink cartridges.

▶ Keep files in big wicker baskets.

▶ At the end of the day, make your plans for the next day – you can begin this on Thursday.

▶ Take short breaks – don't sit at the computer for more than two hours without stretching your legs.

▶ Have nibbles to dip into – fruit and nuts, barley sugars, dried fruit, cashews.

▶ For each feature you work on, keep all the copy and research material such as cuttings and notes in one plastic, labelled folder. That way, you can locate them easily, and you will not lose any of the bits and pieces that could be vital.

I know I've inundated you with tips – yet above all, I want you to relax this weekend. There are no 'shoulds' or 'musts'. Silence your internal critic. Go for achievable goals, and even if you do less than you expected to, don't beat yourself up about it.

It's Friday!

So… you've had the joining instructions. It's time to move on.

On Friday evening I'd like you to just sit, maybe with a glass of wine, or a coffee, herbal tea or mineral water – whatever you enjoy – and allow yourself to relax. This creativity session is a 'sitting' exercise that will release those all-important ideas for magazine features.

Spend quite a long time – could even be up to two hours – just sitting on your sofa or in a comfortable chair thinking, 'what do I want to write about?' You might have some gentle music playing. You need just a pen and notebook at your side.

Think in a light way about the writing you want to do this weekend – the piece, or pieces, you want to write. But don't let any 'musts' or 'shoulds' come into your mind – keep relaxing, floating, and lying back comfortably. You can do this for as long as you like. But at some point ideas will float into your head.

Just keep sitting and thoughts will swim gently in and out of your mind. You'll be thinking what to have for supper… that you haven't cleaned the kitchen… done your ironing… e-mailed a friend… but let these thoughts come and go.

Soon, a different thought will surface, and it will give you an idea of what you want to write about on this weekend course.

They might be, I want to write about…

▶   My weekend trip to Madrid

▶   Being "just a housewife" in the 21st century

▶   My job in a call centre

▶   Taking a gap year at the age of 55

▶   Creating my stamp-size garden

▶   How I manage my illness or disability

▶   Cooking for one on a budget

▶   My needlework hobby – stitching samplers

▶   Tracing my family tree

▶   Being unemployed

▶   How I deal with stress

▶   My relationship with my mother

▶   Living alone

▶   My holiday in Greece

▶   Bringing up my adopted child

▶   My student debt

As soon as these definite ideas come into your head, jot them down.

You'll need to refine the angle, make your idea more specific – but these ideas are the ones to go for. The ones you'll build on this weekend.

And when you've achieved your goal – finished an article and submitted it – you can tick it off! Won't that feel good?

Top tip

Factor in at least a 30-minute stroll each day, maybe around lunchtime, but don't be tempted to go shopping or stop for a coffee. You're on your weekend course! A short walk will re-energise you. Half an hour is about right.

Remember my words: This weekend will be stimulating, energizing, satisfying and successful. All you have to do is prepare, plan – and produce. You don't have to be perfect! Next up is the keynote speech – all you need to do is listen.

2 – What do magazines want?

'Put yourself in the readers' shoes and imagine exactly what it is they want to know.'

~ Nick Gibbs, Future Publishing

It's Friday night, or perhaps Saturday morning. You've settled down with a cup of coffee. You've cleared your weekend diary, shut down your e-mail and turned your phones off. You have everything you need to begin your weekend course. Your kitchen is stocked up with essential supplies – mostly delicious foods! Now you're ready to write. You've thought a bit about the topics you might tackle, and you've jotted down a few ideas. Great!

But before you start, read this chapter. Don't write a word yet! This part of my book is the keynote speech to your writing weekend course. No writing is involved yet – just relax, settle back, and listen. You're not in an uncomfortable chair at a conference centre, or wondering nervously if you're going to have to read your work aloud, or looking around to see if there's really anyone on the course you'll get on with – you're in the comfort of your own home!

This chapter will give you a basic understanding of what magazines want from you as a writer. And the short answer to that is simple: magazines want what their readers want. And when you know what readers want – when you have the insider knowledge, which I'll give you – you'll have a powerful tool that will help you to write successfully for magazines.

What makes magazines special?

Magazines are not school or college textbooks or technical manuals – unless they're highly specialist magazines for dentists or civil engineers. They are small luxuries or indulgences – they're glossy treats, private pleasures.

They're not like newspapers, either. Newspapers, printed on cheap paper and often given away in supermarkets and train stations, are discarded – they're dumped in waste bins and left on trains and buses. But a magazine is an intensely personal, and much more valued, purchase. A magazine subscription is a valued gift. We don't throw magazines away casually, or hand them on to fellow passengers. They're 'ours'. We want to hang on to them.

How they're made special

When you buy a magazine, you buy a brilliantly-designed, expensively-illustrated glossy package of relaxation, entertainment, escapism, advice, inspiration and information – and as important as editors, designers and photographers are, it's you, the writer, who provide the essential content. It's you who provide the relaxation, pleasure and information. Does that mean you have to be a professional 'expert'? Of course, you have to get your facts right, but most magazine readers don't want to read articles by 'experts'. They don't want to be lectured, or reminded of school. They do want to read features written by people who are just like them, who have experienced the same feelings, fears and anxieties.

Readers want articles written by people just like you. At every magazine I have edited (all five of them!) I have found 'gifted amateurs' to be my very best writers – not the so-called experts on the subjects. Mums love to read articles by other mums, not by doctors; people who love holidays in France want to read pieces by fellow francophiles, not collections of tired cliches by travel agents. Yes, it's possible – even desirable – for a writer to be both an expert and have a personal passion for the topic, yet it's the personal piece that wins. Words from the heart succeed every time.

A for Aspiration...

Each issue of a magazine will have many 'touchpoints' to draw readers in – a variety of gateways into the world of pleasure the reader has bought. It could be a writing competition to win a holiday on a Greek island, a special feature on the next generation of computers, with one to win, or a spread about inexpensive, eco-friendly weddings with tips on arranging your own.

But whatever is on the cover, when you buy a magazine, you think, almost subconsciously 'this magazine is me' because it responds to what you're seeking at that time. For example, if you buy a fashion magazine, you may be interested in the clothes featured, but – more importantly – you aspire in a general way to the grooming and style that's spotlighted on the glossy pages. We buy travel magazines to read the articles and drool over the stunning pictures, yet we may not be planning a holiday this year: thanks to the roof that needs to be replaced, or the children demanding money for their foreign vacations, we may not even be able to afford a holiday. When you buy your favourite food magazine, do you try out all of the recipes? Do you do any of them? Probably not – but that's fine; that's how most of us are! We don't do it – but, crucially, we aspire to do it.

... and Addiction!

Though the first women's magazine was published in 1691, it wasn't until the middle of the 19th century that magazines began to be widely bought and read. The first WH Smith station bookstall – selling magazines – opened on Euston station in London in 1848. More people were able to read after the 1879 Education Act, and with train travel they had more time and opportunity to read. They were eager to buy magazines at train stations – and amazingly still are, despite the predictions that electronic publishing would kill off the printed word. Things have changed very little in that sense – before we embark on a journey, we'll often pick up a magazine. The numbers of people reading magazines and looking relaxed and content well outnumber those pounding laptops and looking stressed! Which group would you rather be in?

Yes, magazines and newsletters endure, matching even television, films and books as favourite forms of entertainment. Thankfully, websites and e-magazines have not put the printed magazine in the shade – because you can't curl up on the sofa with a computer. You can't read a website on the bus, or in the supermarket queue.

Many readers get addicted to magazines. I'm a magazine junkie, and have been since I was a small child, when one of my greatest pleasures was to trawl through my grandmother's store of *Woman* and *Woman's Own*. She saved every single issue. When I was nine and ten, I spent my holidays with her at her little terraced house in Wiltshire. Looking back, I realise she was often terribly disappointed by my visits because I had nothing to say to her all day – I'd just be lying on the sofa reading her magazines! I had two piles by my sofa: magazines still to be read, and those I'd devoured. The latter pile grew higher as the day wore on. I can remember her looking in on me now and then, asking if I'd like to take a walk in the sun with her, or meet some neighbours. My selfish answer was always "not yet Gran... I'm reading." But even though she lived alone and would have liked my company, she never told me off. In fact, she encouraged me to read on because it made me happy.

My favourite sections were the Agony Aunt questions and answers, the letters pages, everything about Britain's Royal Family and readers lives. I quite liked the short stories, but not as much as the magazine articles. These seemed 'real' to me, while the short stories were often too sentimental.

The Big Mix

I see most magazines on the market every month and I edit my own – a glossy monthly travel magazine – as well as writing regularly for several other publications. My library has many books about magazine history and craft. I have a few choice covers framed, and I can't visit any country without bringing back a stash of magazines. American ones are my favourites, but I like the Australian, French and Greek ones, too.

So what is it about magazines that makes me – and you – love them so much? It's this: you can be part of their 'club' simply by buying one issue. You can collect them, write to them and be part of their 'family'. You get a feeling that you are part of a group or community – it could be a community of taxi drivers, Christian women, mothers, singles, antique collectors or 20-something clubbers.

When you begin to prepare your pieces, remember that this vital 'club' feel is what readers want. Like all clubs, it's about shared experiences. Often there are shared values too, even though magazines offer a variety of opinions within their pages.

What else do magazines offer?

▶ The 'me' factor – the reader must look forward to getting the magazine or newsletter, confident that there will be something just right for them in it.

▶ Information the reader can use – contact numbers, helplines, pointers readers can use to enhance their lives.

▶ Encouragement in their hobby or interest – which could be the local parish, gardening, parenting, cooking, the local school, antiques, travel or a charity they support.

▶ Inspiration – every magazine or newsletter needs to have a 'feel good' bonus. This could be as simple as tips for dealing with tax worries, or dates when three local gardens will be open to the public. Again, it's information the reader can use.

▶ How to – readers want a feeling that new skills can be gained. In a practical gardening magazine, this could be as simple as how to pot up a container; in a food magazine, how to make the perfect omelette. They can be old skills refreshed or updated, and conveyed in a new way.

Every specialist magazine shares a common factor. It will:

▶ Provide advice on the specialist subject: retirement, food, accountancy, tax, education

▶ Share readers' enthusiasm for the topic – this can amount to a passion

▶ Give benefits – discounts and extra information

▶ Convey new skills – if the magazine is a practical one, perhaps skills on car mechanics or cookery

▶ See the topic from the viewpoint of the enthusiast – with readers' letters and case histories, anecdotes, contact numbers

▶ Add more than a mainstream magazine can do – go into more detail and be more authoritative

▶ Give real value for money – specialist magazines tend to be more expensive than the mainstream magazines

Local magazines, city and county, have these features in common. They:

▶ Inform

▶ Entertain

▶ Help to bind a community together

▶ Act as a marketing tool

▶ Offer a 'club' atmosphere

▶ Provide a platform for different viewpoints

The ads matter, too

The advertising/editorial partnership in a magazine seems hard at first to understand. It's a conundrum: how can paid-for advertising and unbiased editorial features co-exist in the same package? They are strange bedfellows, yet the alchemy works. The advertisements offer essential information – they, too, provide entertainment and inspiration. You have only to look at the advertisements for expensive clothes, cosmetics, food, travel and cars to see that advertising can be an art form in itself.

The Lady is one example of a magazine read primarily for its highly-focused advertising – parents with jobs for nannies, and nannies looking for jobs – yet in an agreeable entertainment package. Any glossy travel or specialist magazine will illustrate the same point. So when you write for magazines, thinking about the advertising factor is essential. This doesn't mean plugging products in your articles, but simply being aware of the kinds of ads your magazine carries – the ads that bring in the money that allows editors to pay you for your feature!

Stairlifts and reading lamps? Or Dior perfume and Clarins skin care? That's an initial check, yet there will be more to it than that. The stairlifts and reading lamps may be accompanied by ads for Caribbean cruises and face lifts, and the Dior perfume and Clarins skin care might be interwoven with ads for children's clothes and yoghurts. So don't make instant judgements on who your reader is – take a little time to build up an 'ads profile'.

Top tip

The principles of writing for magazines haven't changed at all. Computers have made no difference. Being good at English is your trump card as a writer. Having great computer skills comes nowhere near. So don't worry about not being a computer buff. A computer expert with no ability with language will produce a dull unreadable article.

Magazine wisdom

Here is what some publishers have had to say about their magazines.

'We shall be ready to answer all questions you shall vouchsafe to send us.'

~ *The Ladies Mercury*, publisher John Denton, 1693

'A magazine must be... like a party, filled with colour, lifted from the everyday with attractive, intelligent, well known men and women moving through its pages and filled, not with the old fashioned fiction suitable for the cabbie's wife, but with the popular writers of the time.'

~ *Woman's Own*, publisher James Drawbell, 1946

'Magazines are more than just pages. They are a bond between you and the reader. With imaginative ideas, design and writing, you can strengthen the bond so that readers no longer think of the product as just a magazine.'

~ Nick Gibbs, Editorial Director, Future Publishing, 1996

Getting ideas

Now you're beginning to think round what you'll do – it's still Friday evening or Saturday morning, and you haven't quite started the practical part of the course yet, though if you followed the previous chapter's relaxation exercise, you will have some rough ideas mapped out in your notebook. If you were on a weekend course, students would be gearing up for drinks and get-together time now – an activity which can have mixed blessings! Instead, you can begin to be thoughtful... what will suit you for this course?

Maybe you'll have an idea that might interest an editor, but be at a loss as to how to structure your article. You know the length it should be, and you have a good idea of the readership and tone, but are not sure how to arrange your material. These are some guidelines to think about – but don't start writing yet!

The thing about writing for a magazine is that you must be clear about what you want to achieve. You cannot simply sit down and bang out something you're burning to write – it must have a point, and it must fit into the magazine's objectives and tone. Think of your article as a short story – what's the beginning, middle and end? What's the major point? When you've read it, what have you learned? It's not a bad idea to jot down the 'story line' before you begin writing your article.

How will you get your ideas for writing for magazines this weekend? It's a crucial question, because ideas are the genesis of your articles.

You'll have some ready, but if you want more inspiration, you can:

▶ Look through magazines and newspapers and cut out small paragraphs or news flashes (these used to be known as NIBS – news in brief) that interest you, and that could be worth following up.

▶ Listen to the daily news and jot down any item that might appeal to you to write about.

▶ Walk round your town or city, looking at notice boards – those at local markets are often very useful: is someone advertising a cookery class for men or a beginners workshop in magic? These are potential magazine articles for you.

▶ Look at the business sections of Sunday newspapers. For example, *The Mail on Sunday* will have business stories about supermarkets, beauty companies, food manufacturers, and there may be facts, which would spark off an opinion piece. When I read that Anita Roddick was selling The Body Shop to L'Oreal, I did notes for an opinion piece – it seemed sad that the world-famous 'natural' beauty guru was selling to a company whose products seemed to contain additives. Something I read about John Lewis – they own Waitrose – and the way all of its staff are called 'partners' led to an opinion piece on how I decide to shop, which supermarkets we choose and why. The business pages are surprising in their treasure trove of stories which you could expand on for a magazine article.

▶ Look in the 'workplace' sections of national newspapers such as *The Guardian* and *The Times*. They have features about working life – and that's content you could mine. You may find a preview of a change in employment law, new opportunities for working mothers or the over-50s, articles on new courses and new ways of working – any of these you could explore further in an opinion piece.

▶ Make a habit of loitering in charity shops. There could be old books there that could be compared with new ones – for example, a wartime cook-book or an old book on housekeeping or money. This can happen even in chain store bookshops. In Waterstones recently, I saw that the handbook given to American servicemen heading for Britain during WW2 had been re-published. It's a fascinating guide to social habits and customs in pre-war Britain – and points up all of the changes we've seen since then.

Don't try this at home!

Going through your own attic and digging souvenirs out of long-closed cupboards to find topics might not be a great idea – you may just get bogged down in memories!

Feeiling inspired? You better be!

Now's the time to make some more notes in your new notebook. Make notes on your article before you start. Take some thinking time, and just jot down random ideas.

▶ **DECIDE** how you'll break up the piece – with a whole idea in each paragraph. You will find many examples in this course. The idea-in-every-paragraph technique sounds a little crude, but it will help you to focus on getting the thing onto your screen. Write an outline of the paragraphs, and what will go in each.

▶ **NOW** you have the outline – and you've got all your paragraphs out-lined too, albeit roughly. You can use this technique for any piece of magazine writing. You can refine your ideas, add or change them, later. But you do need to draft your chosen options now. Reader's letters, a travel piece, an opinion piece? Now's the time to decide.

Top tip

When you are working on each of your magazine features, keep all the copy, research material, cuttings and pictures for that feature together in one clear plastic folder, labelled with the title. You can buy large labels in sheets from any stationers. I recommend the big labels, as they are clearer to read. Mark them with a felt tip pen in large letters – then you can locate your folder easily, and you will not lose any of the bits and pieces. If you are really organized, you can colour-code your folders: red for women's magazines, blue for travel, yellow for think pieces, and so on. Colour coding really does help organization.

The Ten Commandments of... magazine craft

This is a little taster of the course to come, and it's something to think about as you prepare. By the end of the weekend, you will have completed a body of work. These are the ten golden rules – which we'll expand on as we go through the course:

1   Make it clear why the reader should read your piece. Get the benefit into the first paragraph. Explain the nub of the story. To be engrossed by a feature, the reader needs to know at the start how she or he will benefit. Supplement the main read with tips, do's and don'ts, a factbox. These add-ons add value. Don't worry, more on these later!

2   Include opinions – Don't just mention techniques, products or systems and places: include your opinion. If you test something, give a verdict.

3   Study the ad pages. From the ads, you'll glean an idea of the trends and topics that appeal to the reader of this particular magazine – and you'll be able to gear your language more closely to this reader. Ads could be for cars, cosmetics, food or holidays. They could be lonely hearts or small ads. If they're for stairlifts and health insurance, you're reading a magazine for seniors – but they'll still be interested in travel, grooming and food.

4   Leave no questions unanswered. Whatever your piece is about – health, money, food, shopping, politics – there should be no areas of vagueness. Use plenty of detail; be specific.

5   Think about how the reader feels when he/she buys a magazine. When do you buy one? In your office lunchtime as a treat to look forward to, after an unfulfilling shopping trip, in the supermarket as a luxury after stocking up with the basics, or at the station before a bus or train journey? Magazine readers are definitely looking for diversion – and a form of comfort.

6   Be honest. The more honest you can be on the page, the more chance you have of great success. Be candid about bad experiences as well as good; be honest in your feelings and opinions; be down-to-earth in your advice – and be yourself. Get you and your life onto that page – no matter what topic you're writing about

7   Surprise your readers. They like surprises. Even if you're writing on a well-worn topic, strive for a new and surprising fact. For example, in an article I read recently about the history of money, I learned that the first ever form of cash, discovered in Greece, was kebab sticks – sticks used to grill meat!

8   Do your own original research – don't just plunder the internet. Cuttings from magazines and newspapers help build up your research.

9   Don't use long words when perfectly good short ones will do. Word count should match the typical count in the magazine you're aiming for.

10   Make sure your spelling is correct, and the grammar allows the reader to understand what you're saying – and don't rely on your computer's spelling and grammar check: it won't know the difference between right and write, and the grammar software won't alert you to the problem with this sentence: *The judge, said the accused, was a black-hearted killer and would get the very long prison sentence he deserved.*

Watch your tone

You've got your magazines in front of you, the ones you've bought just for this course, the ones you hope to see your own name in. Study them carefully – study the 'tone' with extra care. All that means is, the way they are written.

You are planning your article for a certain magazine – maybe a woman's or a travel magazine. It is important to carefully 'deconstruct' the style and tone of a magazine – and to follow it, without copying any of the form. It sounds difficult, but begin by reading one piece repeatedly.

Is the style friendly, bossy, self-effacing, serious or neutral? Is it gushing, ironic, nostalgic, cosy, distanced, youthful or jokey? Magazines make a great fuss about 'tone' – it has to be exactly right. For example, if you used *The Sun*'s tone for an article you hope to place in *The Times*, you would not get very far. It's just the same with magazines.

Top tips for crafting

▶ Anything that can be picked out as a coverline – used on the cover – will be even more tempting to the editor you're trying to impress. Use 'number' pieces – 9 can't fail housework shortcuts; 7 things to avoid: 5 easy steps to happiness: 11 stress-free destinations; 3 ways to family harmony. Each point can have at least 200 to 300 words written around it. For some reason, magazines prefer odd numbers to even ones in lists: don't ask me why.

▶ Include tips, hints, box-outs, do's and don'ts. They make the page look good and readers love them. This is known as 'layering' – you have your main article, then a couple of smaller layers to go with it. Each layer expands on something you've said before.

▶ Write to the length of articles you see published in the magazine – not longer, not shorter. You have no option but to roughly count them on the page.

▶ Satisfy readers. Even if they don't have time to read a whole feature, at least include tips, an anecdote, a case study or factfile that will draw them into the piece, and help them feel rewarded.

Where are we now?

So – now you've written a list of possible magazine ideas and you have fleshed them out a little in your notebook. You've studied the background to magazines and what magazines essentially want. Already you know far more than the average person on magazine history!

Now you know about:

▶ The club feel of magazines

▶ The importance of your feature fitting the magazine's word count and 'tone'

▶ Being as honest as you can when you write

▶ The role of ads as well as the articles

▶ 'Number' features – 7 ways to be happier; 6 steps to wealth

▶ Adding 'layers' – extra tips, listings, do's and don'ts

- ▶ Telling readers why they should read your article
- ▶ Including your own opinions
- ▶ Leaving no questions unanswered

Remember – magazines are more than just pages. They are a bond between the title and its reader. Knowing this will help you with your goals this weekend. Now you have some magazine history, magazine rationale and some crafting tips. And remember my mantra: you don't have to be a great writer; you just have to communicate clearly.

Now you're ready to begin! Let's go!

3 – Dear Editor…

'From an editor's point of view, the ideal letter is one that requires no editing whatsoever; it's short, grammatically correct and makes its point succinctly. If it's witty, that's a bonus.'

~ David Kernek, travel magazine editor

Want to start your weekend course with a reader's letter to a magazine of your choice? You can – and will! – write a letter this weekend which will be published. My tricks of the trade have worked for thousands of would-be writers, and they'll work for you.

This session contains all the tools you'll need to get your letter printed. I defy you to follow my advice and not see your letter published! It's certainly a big thrill – there's really nothing quite like it.

My first letter

The very first time I saw my name in print was when I was nine years old. I wrote a letter to a children's magazine called *Girl* – yes it was a few years ago! And the letter talked about how I had decorated the walls of my attic bedroom with full-page pictures cut from *Girl* magazine. In every issue they had a beautiful whole-page photograph – anything from a portrait of Audrey Hepburn to a view of a church or mountain.

I recommended this remarkable interior décor tip to other children who had bedroom walls that needed livening up. Like many rooms in old houses of that time, my bedroom had ancient wallpaper. My parents had stretched themselves enough just buying their own house. This was before the days of instant Ikea and Habitat!

I spent an afternoon pasting 30 or 40 pictures straight on to the faded paper, making a colourful gallery. Then I sat down and wrote my letter on an equally old portable typewriter my dad had used when he was in the RAF during the war.

My prize for this seven-line offering was a postal order that would be worth about £10 in today's cash. My joy knew no bounds. But without knowing it, I'd followed exactly the pattern I would recommend to students years later. It's this – for a good chance of your letter being used, always refer to how the magazine has helped you.

The key is confidence

It's much, much easier to get a reader's letter into a magazine than writers generally think. Get that letter in and besides the pleasure of seeing it there, you could scoop valuable prizes – champagne, cosmetics, books, cookware, hotel weekends away, flowers and foreign travel.

I have edited a number of magazines and I have worked as a staff writer on national glossy magazines. And, guess what? – most magazines rarely have enough good letters to print! Usually my magazine postbags are crammed with letters, but now and again there's a quality shortage. Then I sometimes call readers who have e-mailed me or telephoned me about something, asking them to shape their comments into a letter for publication.

Mostly, they are very surprised and startled. They just hadn't had the confidence to do this themselves, nor had they thought I would be interested. "Is what I say really good enough?" they ask. They'll even ask me to repeat my request… as if they can't believe it.

Good enough? Why would I waste time calling them if it wasn't! All of which supports my premise that lack of confidence – and not fear of rejection – is the basis of lack of success in writing for magazines. Good letters are at a premium!

What makes a good letter?

What's the definition of "good"? You'll meet it exactly if you follow my tips. Basically the usable letter:

▶ Is short – three or four paragraphs at most

▶ Is sent with a picture of the writer

▶ Expresses an emotion

▶ Is succinct

▶ Contains a whole idea

- ▶ Refers to something already printed in the magazine; it might challenge or applaud something that's been printed in a recent issue

- ▶ Offers a tip from the writer's experience

- ▶ Shares something that happened to the reader   good or bad

- ▶ Celebrates a personal triumph over tragedy

Compliments all round

Prizes for reader's letters in women's magazines are excellent. And their letters nearly always refer to a previous issue of the magazine. That's the thing to remember.

So this weekend, as you compose your letter (with your target magazine in front of you!), it's good to:

- ▶ Compliment the mag on a recent feature, but go a bit further – include the name of the writer and say what the feature meant to you. If it was a health feature, was it reassuring or encouraging? A relationship feature outlining a situation you had experienced? A parenting article with tips you could use? Be specific.

- ▶ Pick out five projects or tips from the magazine, which you adopted from the last issue.

- ▶ Name a problem or illness that's worrying you, and ask readers for their advice.

- ▶ Refer to a long-ago issue of the magazine – if you've been collecting the magazine for more than five years – and talk about an idea you still use from it.

- ▶ Talk about how other family members – of different generations – use the magazine.

- ▶ Tell them when and why you subscribed, or bought a gift subscription for a family member or dear friend.

Taking aim

Sigmund Freud famously – or infamously – asked what it was that women wanted. The question we must ask is: what do women's magazines want?

For women's magazines, you need to lock in to the feelings and frailties, which all women share. The more honest you are, the more your voice comes through. Can you be candid about your hopes, fears, triumphs and disasters? Of course you can! The traditional, long established magazines such as *Woman & Home*, *She* and *Good Housekeeping* are always looking for letters that reflect their readers' lives. Few magazines fail to include a letters column – the letters column holds the "identity" of any magazine.

Here are lots of extracts from typical magazine letters, with my comments and notes for you.

▶ *As any student knows, the only way to really remove burnt on stains is to use a biological washing powder tablet – drop it in the pan, fill it with hot water and go and sit on the sofa and watch TV while the washing power does it for you*

~ Lotte Russell, Auchtermuchty – *She*

A perfect offering for the mag's "tips and solutions" section – how to clean a burnt-on pan while sitting on the sofa! It's what *She* is all about. The simplest little tip, written in this lively way, could earn you publication.

▶ *I have to complain about the* Grown-up Woman's Guide to Modern Manners *in* Good Housekeeping. *Never apply make-up in front of a man in case you spoil the fantasy? I don't want him to be in love with a fantasy, I want him to be in love with me! What sort of relationship is it if dishonesty starts with something so simple? And don't talk to people in a lift in case they think you're odd or giving the come on? No! DO Talk to people so they learn conversation is just that. I'm appalled that a forward-thinking magazine peddles these fallacies – please remember feminism, equality and the freedom to be, and lead accordingly,*

~ Becky John, Southampton – *Good Housekeeping*

This letter challenges the magazine. Editors welcome well argued, critical letters that still recognize the magazine as a 'leader'. It's a strong, but not angry, letter. Don't be afraid to take the magazine to task like this – the chances are they'll use your letter! Magazines don't turn down the opportunity to show readers how fair they are, and how they can take criticism.

▶ *Your article on little black dresses brought back memories of my LBD, which now sits at the back of my wardrobe. I bought it for my son's 18th birthday – he is now 38 – and I cannot part with it. It still looks great and friends have borrowed it – one of them even went to the trouble of altering it so it would fit!*

~ Esther Cotterill, Belper, Derbyshire – *Woman & Home*

The writer hits the target readership perfectly – 50-ish and attractive, also careful with clothes and possessions. The old-fashioned values of saving clothes and altering them, instead of buying new, are introduced. You get the feeling that the writer will look glamorous in this dress, and that she will take a lot of trouble with her appearance, in common with the magazine's readership.

► *Last year, approaching 50 and with my daughter flying the nest, I started reading* Woman & Home. *It convinced me that this was no time to curl up by the fire and dream about early retirement. Instead, I've started an accountancy course and have learned to ski. I've been inspired and have no intention of slowing down any time soon.*

~ Marija Lees, Exeter, Devon – *Woman & Home*

This magazine boasts "a brand new attitude", and the editor's view is that it's not age which defines us, but attitude. *Woman & Home* readers are adventurous, and youthful in looks and personality. They see mid-life as a chance to try new things, as this writer so aptly demonstrates. Use of the word 'inspired' is just right; all magazines aim to be inspiring.

► *This is the second issue of* Red *that I have bought and I can't put it down. It's as if you have got into my head and written exactly what I've been thinking about. Over the past few months my partner and I have been researching into investing in property abroad: so it was great to hear other people's experiences in Fly to Let. The article that had the biggest impact was Want To Start Your Own Business? I want to set up my own company but I'm apprehensive. Thanks to you I am determined to research my idea, enter your competition and subscribe to your magazine. And that's not all. Your beauty pages have given me the incentive to change my hairstyle too*

~ C Anderson, Lancashire – *Red*

There are some great phrases here to use in your letters: "can't put it down"; "written exactly what I've been thinking about"; "and that's not all"; and "given me the incentive". The writer also says she'll subscribe and she'll enter the magazine's competition for business ideas. In your letter, offer the impression that the magazine has read your mind – they'll love it!

> ▶ *If you have a zip that won't open or close easily, there's no need to replace it. Instead, rub a soft pencil up and down the zip's teeth. The graphite in the lead acts as a lubricant and the zip should run freely again. But don't try this with white jeans.*
>
> ~ Suzy Braun, Leeds – *Prima*

Two useful tips in one – how to get a zip going again, and how not to ruin a pair of white jeans! If you can expand your tip like this, you add extra value – and more chance of publication. Write your tip – and then add a tiny bit more.

> ▶ *I'd love* Good Housekeeping *to lead the way in taking a different approach to Christmas. Levels of debt in this country are such that people don't need to be encouraged to waste money. It would be better given to those who do need it, whether in this country or abroad, while the donors acknowledge the spirit of goodwill with home made gifts and modest eating and drinking in the company of people they actually like. As every magazine seems to get round to saying sooner or later, that's what counts.*
>
> ~ Fen Crosbie, Edinburgh – *Good Housekeeping*

This is similar – a thoughtful opinion, and one you might not share at a Christmas party, but could express in print. The topic of saving cash and resources – both personally and globally – is a hot one. Create a letter around this subject and you could be onto a winner. Magazines are sometimes criticised for encouraging wasteful consumer spending and they like the opportunity to present the opposite view.

> ▶ *I just wanted to say how much, as a harried mum of two small children, I appreciate the fashion in* Eve. *It's consistently gorgeous, inspirational and far less frumpy than in the magazine I'd previously bought. My wardrobe thanks you for all your help.*
>
> ~ Sophia Phillips, London – *Eve*

This follows the winning formula – compliment the magazine, but your applause must be sincere. Always give an example of how the advice helped you. The thanks coming from the wardrobe – that's a bit different, adds an original touch.

> ▶ *I make a date for myself every week or two, and actually pre-book a ticket to an art exhibition, or a film that I know my husband wouldn't want to see. You're more likely to do it if you book in advance and then actually write the date in your diary.*
>
> ~ Maureen Leese, Blackburn – *She*

The magazine asked readers to tell them how they created 'me time'. This was one of the successful letters. It offers an original tip a reader could follow the next day. Every magazine wants these type of letters – readers crave ideas to make their lives more relaxing, less stressful, with time they can slice out of their busy diaries that's just for them. I read this and followed the advice the very next day – booked a film ticket for a movie I knew my partner would run a mile to avoid, but I'd drool over.

> ▶ *Surely there isn't a straight yes or no answer to the question you posed in September's Debate "Should restaurants scrap reservations?" As a simple generalization, the more expensive the restaurant, the more need there is for a booking system. So, for example, Le Gavroche: yes, Pizza Express, no.*
>
> ~ Robert Shaw, East Molesey, Surrey – *Waitrose Food Illustrated*

A touch of humour or irony can work very well in a reader's letter for certain magazines. And this little letter makes a very good point – often there is no straight yes or no to dilemmas posed by magazines. So adapt this letter to create your own viewpoint.

> ▶ *I really liked your floral arrangement in a teacup and saucer idea for Mother's Day. Instead of a Mother's Day gift, I made one for my sister- in- law's 40th birthday and she loved it. It's such a simple idea but so effective.*
>
> ~ Gill Bonnamy, Aberdeen – *Prima*

Prima has always been the "makes" magazine – its readers love their crafts. Any magazine likes to know its ideas are simple to do and bring pleasure.

> ▶ *I've just been reading through dozens of my mother's recipes, saved from magazines from the 50s to the present day. I never realized how much our attitude to cookery has evolved in the span of a single lifetime.*

> *Thrift dominated the recipes of the 1960s and 1970s. We were endlessly shown how to stretch our budget as far as possible, as in your feature that reveals How To Feed Six people for a Tenner. So much seems to have been possible with what was a limited range of ingredients; this was before the days of imported fruit and veg. My favourite, though, is a pamphlet from the Potato Marketing Board – Keep Slim with Potatoes. This was obviously before the days of Dr. Atkins.*

> ~ James McDonald, Malvern, Worcestershire
> *– Waitrose Food Illustrated*

Practical nostalgia is often a winner, especially when it's about food. Use plenty of detail. What books and magazines do you collect? Is this a theme you could adapt for your letter this weekend?

▶ *At 8 a.m. on a cold and damp day in February, I'm not normally at my best – especially when I have only finished work some seven hours previously (I'm a publican with a 1 a.m. licence)*

> *So with a cup of strong coffee in my hand I set about sorting the morning post. With bleary eyes I was sifting through far too many envelopes with windows.*

> *And there it was under yet more bills, the March issue of* Greece *magazine. The sun started shining and I started to warm up – from then on things only got better.*

> *Crete is special – that's where Hellenic Homes have just finished our beautiful house. Drive to Greece? That's what we are hoping to do – my thanks to Jos Simon for the advice and the very good website. But the icing on the cake was seeing my letter to Hellenic thanking them for their excellent work. I think the expression on my face in this photo tells it all. So on behalf of my customers, who for today at least will see a happy smiling face behind the bar, thank you* Greece *magazine!*

> ~ Stefan Pollard, Deal – *Greece Magazine*

I picked this as my star letter in an issue of *Greece* magazine. Stefan had sent a clear, smiling, informal picture of himself holding up the magazine! His letter ticked all the boxes. It was irresistible. He'd written so naturally about his work and his feelings. He'd mentioned all the reasons why the magazine is an award-winner with a huge subscriber base. He won a copy of *The Rough Guide to Greece*, worth £14 99!

▶ *Fanny Blake gave great advice in* Would You Buy in Spain? *(June,* Woman & Home*). Having done it myself, I'd say the most important tip is to rent first. People just tend to think of sun and sangria, but in winter it can be cold, with torrential rain and many houses have insufficient heating. Life in Spain is different outside the holiday season and one can feel homesick when the novelty wears off. My husband and I didn't rent before we bought and realized that life in Spain wasn't for us. Fortunately, we'd kept a little place in England – another important thing to do before you buy abroad.*

~ Barbara A Williams, Surrey – *Woman & Home*

This writer understands the power of 'I made the same mistake', linked with useful advice from her own bitter experience. When you join in with ' I did it too', always offer tips so that readers don't fall into the same trap, whatever that may be. Your mistake could be anything – from taking the wrong job for the wrong reasons to going out with the wrong guy or buying the wrong type of holiday. But give ideas for readers on getting it right.

▶ *I've had a subscription to* Woman & Home *for the last four years as a Mother's Day gift. Two years ago, my son-in-law's job took him, my daughter and three precious grandchildren to New York. For her first birthday away from home, my daughter asked for a subscription to* W&H *as she really missed it. We now e-mail and phone regularly and* W&H *articles are always discussed. We love the fashion, gardening and "new directions" features. So thank you* W&H *– somehow the miles between us seem less now we both read the same magazine!*

~ Maureen Williams Surrey – *Woman & Home*

An excellent letter, which won her a luxury weekend at a Scottish hotel. Don't just say 'I'm a subscriber and I love it', but give examples of how being a subscriber has enhanced your life. The detail about the subscription as a regular Mother's Day gift is another winner. Detail, detail, detail – it's key to winning letters. Plus that essential little picture of you!

▶ *As a keen fisherman, I'd like to thank you for your article on fishing, in the last issue, in which you make an excellent point – why shouldn't more women enjoy it? The young lady you interviewed says she loves it because it's relaxing and gives her a chance to enjoy the countryside. I'm hoping her comments will help to persuade my two daughters to give it a try.*

~ Alex Mackay, Co Waterford – *Holiday Cottages magazine*

The feature was about the Environment Department's push to promote fishing as a hobby for women. But rather than simply saying he enjoyed it, the writer goes a bit further and says he hopes his daughters will give it a try. Pick a topic that's not one of the lead features from a magazine – this was a minor piece – and write a letter on that. As there will be far less competition, your letter is likely to be used.

> ▶ *I hated wearing glasses because they made me feel geeky and unattractive. I never wore makeup or made an effort with my appearance – what would have been the point? When I was told to wear glasses at 18, I was devastated. If there was a boy I fancied or if I went on a date, I'd take off my glasses and try to navigate with blurry vision. I did start wearing contact lenses but I wore them so often I made my eyes sore. So it was back to wearing glasses – and back to feeling frumpy. But last year all that changed [when she had laser eye surgery].*
>
> ~ Anna Maria Cutronem – *Prima*

Wearing glasses has blighted many a young woman's life – or she's felt it has. I know it did when I was a teenager, but I thought things had changed, and that women didn't worry so much now. Wrong! It's still the same – otherwise why would laser eye surgery be so popular? Why do women still snatch their glasses off when they see a man they like? Why do we torture ourselves trying " to navigate with blurred vision"? This writer picks up these feelings perfectly, as well as giving useful info about the eye laser procedure. Have you invested in something that has changed your appearance? It could be as simple as wearing different shoes. Write about that. Be this candid about a subject many people are interested in, and the magazine will snap up your letter.

All of those examples I've used will give you a sound idea of the ingredients of successful letter writing.

Top tips for winning letters

▶ The shorter and more succinct your letter, the better the chance of it being published

▶ Always attach a little picture of you to your letter, even if you're sending your letter by e-mail. It's another aid to publication. A clear passport-size picture, preferably smiling, is enough. Look on the pictures as non-returnable – so get a few copies made.

▶ Use e-mail if the magazine accepts it. E-mailed letters save the editor or sub editor time. In busy offices they might be read before the snail mail letters are looked at. Check this weekend what the magazine accepts – if it's happy with e-mail, you can send your letter the minute it's finished.

▶ When you're writing about a topic covered in an earlier edition, give the date of the issue – for example: *I couldn't disagree more with Diana Cambridge when she tells visitors to Greece to tip waiters generously (June)*. Again, this saves time for busy editors – and the less time they have to give to your letter, the better your chance of getting it accepted.

Don't:

▶ Go for poetic language – use plain English

▶ Be angry – be critical

▶ Be sentimental – be sincere

▶ Preach – just advise

▶ Pretend – be honest

More letter tips

▶ If you're sending a letter by snail mail, add a short note saying you'd be able to e-mail it too.

▶ When posting your letter, type it and sign your name clearly.

▶ Always give your full address, daytime and evening phone numbers, and e-mail address. If the magazine thinks something in your letter needs clarifying, they'll want to contact you. They might also think your letter is so interesting that it's worth building up into a feature.

Ready… steady… write!

Look through your magazines now and re-read the articles, looking for those you think would make good topics for your letters. If you follow all of my tips, I'd be very surprised if you didn't succeed.

If you can send more than one letter to more than one mag this weekend, you'll widen the scope for success. But – a warning – don't send the same letter to different magazines. Letters must be original.

And a final thought – while your favourite magazine is in front of you and you're composing your letter, fill in the subscription form and treat yourself. You'll enjoy the reader gift that's offered as the subscription bait, and the next magazine that drops on your doormat could contain a letter written by you. You wouldn't want to miss that, would you?

Now you know… how to get your letter published in a magazine.

4 – Opinions please!

'Opinions are clearly distinguished from fact. More than one side of an argument is presented, or at least acknowledged. The reader has a fair chance to judge the reliability of the information.'

~ Arthur Plotnik, *The Elements of Editing*

You've managed a reader's letter this weekend? That's great – you're half way to an opinion piece! But even if you didn't take the letters option, you can still tackle the opinion piece as a stand-alone alternative.

You can do it in one day. It's the simplest to try because:

▶ You need no interviewees – it's just your opinion.

▶ No extensive research is needed – you can put together an opinion piece based on one accurate fact, for example. Your writing skills are all you need.

▶ Think pieces are short – they need be no more than 350 words – and certainly no longer than 750 words.

▶ They can be on very uncomplicated topics – issues that might seem trivial yet concern many readers, such as the value of local Post Offices threatened by closure, or – an ever-popular topic – dog mess on pavements.

▶ There's no shortage of topics – it could be about something that's in the news this week, an issue of current concern locally or nationally such as climate change, an updated take on subjects that always generate controversy, such as divorce, abortion, genetically modified foods and fox hunting, or old favourites such as crime and punishment and men who show more interest in football than in their families.

▶ You don't have to be an expert to write one.

▶ They're never out of fashion. They're always in demand. As more and more people get their hard news from television, radio and the internet, magazines – and newspapers – are publishing more opinion and comment features than ever before. In many ways, the opinion piece is the lifeblood of a magazine or a newspaper, just as they were when the printing press was invented. They're the features that generate response from readers – ensuring that the letters' pages are never empty. Supermarket magazines publish opinion features, too.

Finding your topic

How do you start? The first step is to settle on a subject – pick one that you feel passionate about. Or annoyed or concerned about. It needn't be negative. It could be about something in the news that excited your enthusiasm. Many people – especially those living a long way from London – didn't welcome the decision to give the 2012 Olympic Games to the capital city. Perhaps you did. If so, write a piece explaining why.

But, like it or not, grumbling is a popular British pastime, so the majority of opinion pieces published – and enjoyed by readers – tend to be complaints of one kind or another. I've done grumbly think pieces about:

▶ Those annoying train announcements where they list every sandwich but forget to tell you where the train stops

▶ Boring round-robin letters

▶ Music played in the office at work – it incenses me

▶ Recorded telephone responses – the impossibility of speaking to anyone at a bank

▶ Cold call telephone selling

But I've also written upbeat think pieces on:

▶ How good it is to have European coffee shops now in all our cities

▶ How my life has been improved by home deliveries for groceries

▶ Cheap airline travel – it can be the gateway to weekend happiness

▶ Supermarket offers – where you buy one, get one free

▶ 3 for 2 book offers – great value for book-lovers

These are extracts from three of my own opinion pieces – all published in *The Lady*:

Does the word "clarity" or the phrase "plain English" hold no meaning for rail companies? Their favourite word "sorry" does not to seem to cover the distress they cause, both by endless delays and by inadequate information. For my last three simple rail journeys – two from Bath to Cardiff and one from Bristol to Bath – the trains I intended to catch were all cancelled. Each time, an announcement heralding the arrival of the next appropriate train was larded over with confusing sentences...

When I suggested to a member of the staff that the announcements be made with more clarity, the man spluttered, "They can't, it's a computer!". Yet the inadequacy of the station announcements contrasted with the eagerness with which the staff grab the microphone on the train. During one journey from London to Bath, I listened to the lengthy list of sandwiches six times: there were endless "warm welcomes to the service" from the attendant, all from a sound system which was far too loud and intrusive. Rail staff should be taught that the description of a cheese and tomato sandwich does not need to carry as much weight as the fact that the delayed train to Exeter will now depart from a different platform. Money spent creating inedible sandwiches might well be routed to this.

* * *

Last year my Christmas and New Year mail contained four circular letters – one from a family member, one from a much loved friend and two from business acquaintances I had not seen for years. My feeling (as I read the letters from the business people) was that of a reluctant intruder. I was irritated at having to take in so much detail about people I did not know – was I supposed to react, feel sorry about illnesses, be envious of exotic holidays and brilliant exam results? Yet even as these thoughts went through my head, I followed them by feeling guilty for my sour response... it is as if life has turned into a vast 'chat room' where comments from anyone are invited just for the sake of it. Letters should be personal, should entertain and inspire.

* * *

'Fat Friday!" The young man at my desk waved a notebook at me. At my surprised look, he repeated "Fat Friday?" The explanation was that Fridays had been chosen by my office as a day when a junior would be sent out for special food – bacon sandwiches, chocolate flapjacks and other treats. I gratefully ordered a hot chocolate and a chocolate croissant. It left me wondering

when snack food became so important at work. When I started my career in the 70s, food was not an issue…we had a good three-course meal for about the equivalent of 40p and lunch lasted one and a half hours. Fed this well, we needed no other snacks during the day. Without proper lunch, the office safaris for chocolate bars, crisps, sweets and fizzy drinks or costly "designer" coffees last all day, or so it seems. Now everyone must do the tasks of two or three people. Lunch is down to an average 27 minutes. Given our hard and profitable work, I think that for employers to provide modest on-site food cheaply or free is not so much to ask.

Here's an example from another writer, Celia Brayfield, commenting in *The Lady* on mid-life traumas:

Crisis is such a negative word. It means disruption, shock, trauma, chaos. A crisis is a bad thing and a mid-life crisis… well, we tend to think of that as the worst thing that can happen…with a mid-life trauma you not only get trauma but ridicule…nothing good can come of a mid-life crisis – or can it?

She goes on to conclude…

… the truth is that although we may feel that time is running out, we still have plenty of it left. For us, 50 is the age of bop-till-you-drop early retirement plus lots of tender loving care – because we're worth it. A mid life crisis can be a way of reclaiming your life after a phase of socially-approved self-sacrifice.

As I hope these examples demonstrate, your thoughts can't be hurled down randomly, however angry, passionate or enthusiastic you feel about the topic. Like any other piece of journalism, the opinion or comment piece must be structured clearly and logically, enabling the reader to follow you effortlessly and enjoyably from one paragraph to the next. The reader will no more persevere through a jumble of seemingly unconnected statements and assertions than he or she would listen to a drunk ranting on a street corner.

That is one of the golden rules for the opinion piece. Here are some more:

▶ Decide what you want to say – what your point is – before you start writing.

▶ Make just one point, not 15. You're aiming for a short comment, not an essay for a degree course.

▶ If your opinion is based on facts, ensure that you've got the facts right. If you're commenting on the way in which a member of the Royal Family wasted money by flying first class to Spain – that's fine; it's a free country! But if Prince Whatsisname got there by easyJet, your argument is blown out of the water, along with your credibility.

▶ If you're using statistics – for example, the cost of the National Health Service – to support your opinion, you should attribute them and keep the original information handy, in case an editor wants to make sure that you haven't just made them up!

▶ Be succinct – do not use ten words when the same work can be done just as well by five.

▶ Don't be pompous – you're not writing a church sermon. Use humour whenever possible.

▶ Choose the opening words with extra care – these are the words or phrases that will grab the reader's interest, or send them off to another article – or sleep! *"Fat Friday!"* is much more likely to get the fickle reader's attention than: 'When I was at my desk in the office, a young man with a notebook…'

▶ Don't go in for anger or personal abuse (although ridicule is OK) – and get a basic grasp of the law of libel. If you say someone is a liar, or a crook – or if you say anything that could damage his or her reputation – you and the magazine could face legal action. This could result in large fines and massive legal bills unless you can prove that what you've written is true or fair comment. Most libel cases are lost by writers and publishers!

Nothing quite like The Lady

A national weekly magazine open to both men and women writers – and in my opinion, one of the easiest to get into – is *The Lady*. Britain's oldest surviving women's magazine (it was founded in 1885) it's almost the only national publication which still welcomes and uses contributions from untried freelances,

Not strictly a " magazine", it describes itself as a newspaper, and this is its key element. Opinion pieces you send to *The Lady* must be topical or news-related in some way – based on anniversaries, current controversies, new research or new exhibitions.

The key word is 'new', although, the new will often have a bearing on the old. Points of view are always welcome. These often take a facet of modern life – mobile phones, the rail service, the postal system, banking, shopping, education – and contrast it unfavourably with how things were done in the past. But not always – you may have a point of view applauding something modern and comparing it to the bad old days.

The Lady receives hundreds of submissions from hopeful freelances every month. Ninety per cent of these are rejected. Its editor is very clear about what the magazine wants from freelance contributors: "Something that is well written, well researched, absolutely accurate with all facts checked, and original." Fact checking is paramount – the magazine will not accept a second piece from a writer who makes a mistake.

The editor points to published pieces on personal safety, phobias and paths to happiness as perfect pieces for *The Lady*. But it's hard – even for me! – to put into words just what that indefinable *Lady* factor is.

It's best to explain by example. This is Janie Jackson, writing in *The Lady* in 2005:

> *It is only recently that I have been driven to scream at the television screen. It is not the programmes that infuriate me – though goodness knows they are bad enough – it is the newsreaders, interviewers and presenters. There was a time when anyone who broadcast on radio or television spoke impeccably. I feel like shouting "Come back Alvar Liddell, all is forgiven".*

Why did I pick that example? Of all readerships, *The Lady*'s is the one most likely to care about clear speech – and quite right too. Personally, I can't stand people who mumble, talk too fast or won't speak clearly, but I'd be pretty careful where I admitted that. Snobbish? Me? *The Lady* would be the right journal for my views, but presented in a non-angry way. Alvar Liddell was a BBC radio newsreader when the radio was better known as the wireless, and he had a cut glass English accent. His voice would be very out of place, far too "posh" on radio or television today. The writer says she screams at the TV screen, but there's a touch of humour here, so we know, or hope, she isn't screaming in a psychotic way. An educated, well argued moan is just right for *The Lady*.

Here's another example, again from *The Lady*. Valerie Haddad was writing about safety belts on coaches:

> *The importance of wearing seat belts was very much on my mind during my recent holiday in Edinburgh with a well-known travel company. One of the highlights on offer was a visit by coach to Glamis Castle. To my dismay and to that of some of my fellow travellers, many seat belts on the coach were found to be faulty.*

This is a simple safety point of view that works well. Safety is a hot topic in the 21st century – many companies will not invest in it, putting people's lives at risk. Yet a feature written in an abstract or too-technical way about seat belts has the potential to be dull. The writer talks about her coach trip "with a well-known travel company" and the lack of working seat belts, and goes on to link this to coach accidents in which people not wearing belts had been injured. A slightly indignant, yet not angry, point of view works well here. Your tone should be one of reasonable, well-argued criticism; *Lady* readers can be dismayed, but never gobsmacked.

The simple opinion works for other successful magazines, too. This is Sandy Boler, writing in *Woman & Home* about her bed:

Perhaps I read too many Hans Christian Anderson tales when I was a child. Or maybe not enough. Either way, the Princess and the Pea was one story that really took my fancy. Freud apart, it could explain why to this day, my bed is my favourite place, dressed with care according to the seasons.

Sandy goes on to talk about how much she loves her bed and her bedroom – Freud apart, there's no sex here – and the feeling of drifting off to sleep. But because it's a title with Home in it, she also talks about the pleasure of buying new bedlinens – crisp new sheets and duvet covers. This is for anyone who has ever thought, "this is lovely" when they wearily get into bed at the end of a tough day – and that's all of us, I suspect. It's such a simple, but universal, theme. For the women's magazine market, you can link an opinion with your home.

Trade tricks

Here are some more tricks of the opinion writing trade:

- **GENUINELY** useful features for women are at a premium. Safety, economy, buying property, management of leisure time, solo travel – can you find an opinion that gives a new twist on any of these?

- **STRONG** opinion? *The Lady* uses a viewpoint every week. Present a clear argument, with a whole idea in each paragraph. Don't be offensive or over-sentimental. Read *Daily Mail* leader articles for a sense of style and tone.

- **DON'T** be afraid to challenge conventional, received or fashionable opinion. It's assumed that everyone hates modern architecture. But perhaps you can think of five modern buildings you wouldn't want to see knocked down? Or perhaps you believe there's nothing wrong with top footballers and tennis players earning zillions of pounds a week. Most editors will always give slightly off-beat or surprising opinions a second look.

- **READ** magazine opinion pieces every week or month, but do not send in copycat ideas or try to follow up a piece. All magazines want original work, and will not be interested in your views on a topic it's just covered – unless you've a very different angle on it.

- **LOOK** to the world of work for topics for opinion pieces: job sharing, working from home, job shadowing, flexi-time, using foreign languages at work, coaching and training, desktop publishing, the virtual office and temping

- **IF** you strike gold and have an acceptance, follow up your success quickly. Send fresh ideas straight away. Once you are tried, tested and trusted, you could become one of the magazine's regular writers.

While you don't have to be an expert to write an opinion or viewpoint piece, specialist knowledge can give your comment added weight or authority – something editors and readers will respect. Here are four fashionable areas for features that combine comment and advice:

▶ **FINANCE** – investment and pension planning – if you are knowledge-able (perhaps you have retired from banking or building society career) you could find a spot in your local newspaper or senior citizens newsletter.

▶ **FOOD** – A column geared at local people, with local produce and dishes mentioned, and advice on buying, cooking, and serving good food, perhaps with wine suggestions. If you are a confident cook, or have cooked commercially – and have opinions about organic food or the fate of local grocery stores threatened by supermarkets – this could be your arena.

▶ **CITY GARDENS** – more and more people want small patios, terraces or roof gardens. They need ideas on container planting, robust patio plants, herbs and fragrant flowers. If you are a gifted gardener, could you help beginners, offering opinions on what should and shouldn't be grown and promoting the view that a large garden is unnecessary?

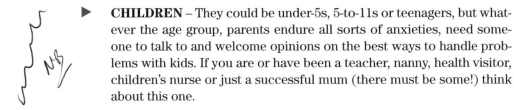

▶ **CHILDREN** – They could be under-5s, 5-to-11s or teenagers, but what-ever the age group, parents endure all sorts of anxieties, need some-one to talk to and welcome opinions on the best ways to handle prob-lems with kids. If you are or have been a teacher, nanny, health visitor, children's nurse or just a successful mum (there must be some!) think about this one.

It's good to be grey

Magazines for older people – the growing number of over-55s – are set for success. More women's magazines, especially, recognize and celebrate the 'grey power' trend and the spending power it represents. There are more active over-55s today than there have ever been – and they love magazines. They are also more likely than younger people to have strong and coherent opinions and an intelligent understanding of news and current affairs. They might change the way they vote from one election to another, but they have formed political opinions and attitudes. They have something to say – and they like to hear other people's views, possibly to challenge them, maybe to agree.

This is an example from *The Bath Magazine*, written by Peter Woodward. A trustee of the Bath Preservation Trust, he argues that the city must be continually vigilant in preserving Bath's architectural heritage. His tone is persuasive and reasonable, yet with undeniable passion.

He begins:

> *In Bath, architecture assaults your senses everywhere. Yet no one in their right mind would think of coming here to seek out good, modern buildings. There aren't any. Well, hardly any.*

He continues:

> *...let us look first at the good things of the last 50 years. As I am now older than the Queen, I can easily cast my mind back to the war years when I was a student at Bristol University. Bath then, quite apart from the horrors of the Baedeker raids, was a coal-black run-down city of decaying stonework and peeling paint from its much-altered windows. I stared in disbelief that it could look so uncared-for. Did no one realise what a jewel there was in this glorious setting?*

There are only seven paragraphs in this first class opinion piece. Peter talks about the achievements in Bath in the last half century, but also

> *... the bad news... The exceedingly controversial demolitions of the late 60s and 70s generated rebuilds that were generally unsatisfactory and created new problems. The icons of the period are so universally disliked that I see no need to vote for any of them as Bath's worst building.*

He talks of "the sting in the tail" – government and council preservation grants to householders have been withdrawn – and concludes with a paragraph nominating his best modern building. He avoids the trap of saying that no modern building in Bath is worthy of a mention. His opinion is forceful – but without anger.

The matter of fact yet elegant way he writes includes phrases such as:

No one in their right mind

There aren't any

Hardly any

Exceedingly controversial

Generally unsatisfactory

Older than the Queen

He's writing as he might talk to someone. Maybe over a meal, yet with a little more precision, keeping the way the words look on paper in mind. You can do this with any of your opinions, on any topic. You can use forceful, literate phrases such as "sting in the tail" or "no one in their right mind" because they express exactly an idea. But you'll avoid weary cliches such as "gone pear-shaped" or "watch this space" because that's just what they are – weary.

So, now you know all about opinion pieces – write one!

5 – It's a goal!

*'Observe that you are to be your own best friend
– not simply your stern and disciplinary elder'*

~ Dorothea Brande, *Becoming a Writer*

Take a break from your desk for a while. This is your coaching session; your relaxation slot. It's your time for a writing boost; an injection of confidence. It's your essential self-esteem boosting break – the pep talk, the personal encouragement, you'd have from a tutor on any good residential weekend course.

Don't miss this chapter – you'll never regret the time spent reading and thinking about it.

You, the coach

In my experience, writers need confidence boosting as much as they need practical information. A rejection slip, or just a discouraging throwaway remark from a friend, can be devastating.

Even a downturn in physical energy can result in you thinking, 'Am I up to it? Is it worth going on, or shall I just rest and read a book?'

Then there's the notorious writer's block, when you're stuck for hours in front of your computer. Nothing comes out; it's so difficult to shape an idea or squeeze out a coherent sentence. That's when boredom, loneliness and, at its worse, despair can set in.

All writers encounter these experiences. But there is a way around them: you need to become your own writing 'coach'. It's the DIY approach: coach yourself. When there's no one else around to help when things don't go well, be your own cheerleader; encourage yourself in your writing. She's always on your side. All her comments are constructive and encouraging; she doesn't judge. You can be that coach!

This weekend, I want to strengthen your resolve, enhance your confidence and energise you, so that you can concentrate far more on your writing and far less on those feelings of not being a good enough writer to ever get published... or even of just not being good enough!

If self-coaching is new to you, don't dismiss it. At least read through this chapter; read about my experience with the 'automatic' goal list. See if, and how, it works for you.

You've got absolutely nothing to lose, and everything to gain!

Goals unlimited

You might have guessed that I'm a huge fan of personal coaching, and of setting goals. I'll tell you why. The short explanation is: it worked for me! Here's how it worked.

Ten years ago, the company I worked for ran into trouble and closed the magazine I edited. Without my well-paid, full-time job, and with no freelance work, I had no other income sources apart from a part-time, £4-an-hour job in a Brighton call centre. I had large debts and a mortgage. What seemed worst of all, I was 45-plus.

I sat down alone by the sea, and wrote 40 goals for myself. I'd read a book called *Write It Down, Make It Happen*, by Henriette Anne Klauser (Simon & Schuster £10) and this was what she'd advised.

Some goals seemed impossible, quite out of reach, crazy, at the time, but they just raced from my pen. I wrote them very rapidly, as she'd urged, without thinking very deeply about them.

I did this on that morning by the sea all those years ago. Today, I can say that 30 of those goals have been achieved, including 20 directly related to writing and publishing.

I've achieved many of those which, when I wrote them down, seemed totally unattainable.

Own a home in Greece was one – but I had no money for a second home! I couldn't even afford to live in the one I had! But three years later I was offered the incredible opportunity to create, launch and edit a glossy travel magazine about Greece, and eight years on I was viewing studios and apartments in Athens.

Here's another goal on that list: *a column in a national newspaper*. I'd never come near one. I'd had some features published in national newspapers and magazines, but now my career was on the skids. But those were the words that fell from my pen. Three months later I was contributing columns on office life regularly to *The Guardian* and *The Times*.

And another... *a regular newspaper feature about ordinary people and their work*. Two months later, the *Brighton Argus* 'phoned me – yes, they liked my idea for a weekly feature, and would I do it?

Would I do it? My first piece was about working in a Brighton call centre – based on my own experiences. I was actually working in one the day they called me! This was one of the lowliest jobs I'd ever had, but I was working with some of the nicest people I had ever been with, so I'll never regret having to take this job. Now that £4-an-hour job was helping me to generate more much-needed income – in earnings from freelance writing.

As I racked up more and more work – pounding my computer from a desk in a tiny hallway because our flat was so small – I realized to my delighted amazement that I was marching steadily but surely down my goal list.

I still am. It still works.

But there's nothing that special about me – except for my passion for goals, coaching and magazines. Although I do now have an invaluable professional coach, Michael, whose services I pay for every three months or so, I have learned to be my own coach, which is the ultimate aim of coaching.

My goals have become more ambitious. I am no longer scared of success, and I'm prepared to do a lot to get it. I accept that now and again I become despondent, stressed, even angry – but I've learnt that these moments can be survived. I don't dwell on depression; I have trained myself to ignore it.

Write on auto

Can you write an 'automatic' goal list for yourself? Will you?

I recommend you try it. In a quiet time, in a quite place – maybe on this writing course weekend – sit down with a notebook and pen. Let your pen take off on its own, writing down your goals. Do not agonize over them; don't stop to edit or amend them. Give in to the flow. Don't think about them; this is automatic writing. Let the thoughts spring from your brain, and write down whatever comes out.

It's a project that takes a certain amount of spiritual energy – only do it if you can put in the time, and are prepared for the results!

Your writing objectives will most certainly appear on your list. Keep the paper with the written goals on in a very safe place. Success won't happen overnight – but it will happen. Soon you'll be ticking off your first goal.

In writing your goal list, you will have taken the first step towards becoming your own coach. Let your coach guide you on. She can urge you into action when you have slumped. She can help when you've become stressed, depressed or angry, without judging the emotions that took you there. She can remind you that your time is finite, and that for a writer, now is the time, the only time.

For me, this fact becomes more real, more urgent. One of my dear friends, writer Crysse Morrison, often reminds me of Goeothe's quote:

> *"Boldness has magic in it."*

You can be bold! Make these writing goals for yourself.

Do the goal list

It's my belief that anyone can adopt a goal-focused, project-led way of life, and that writers more than most people have to. Who else will believe in us? How else can the isolated writer get things done? How else to avoid the despair of the writer when he or she is neither taken seriously nor understood?

As well as your own big goals, which you'll achieve unconsciously, pick weekly and monthly goals, either from my suggestions (below) or from your own lists.

When you achieve your weekly goals, tick them off. Celebrate them. Weekly goals shouldn't be too arduous, though embarking on them will mean changing your routine, making that shift from what's familiar to what seems to call for effort. But once you've started, the effort is replaced by pleasure. Try it for yourself!

When you are ready, when you've begun to see that weekly goals are working for you, you can begin monthly and then annual goals. In a bored or depressed moment – turn to your notebook, and within a while you might see that you are working on one of your listed goals without realizing it. Never wallow in negative thoughts, but use the time to get those feelings down on paper. In even a short time, you'll find your negative thoughts will turn into ideas for things you could write.

It's essential to keep a goals and coaching notebook – you've already bought a spiral-bound one for the weekend. Your notebook, in a way, is you – and it doesn't matter whether you use it for a shopping list or a novel outline, as long as you keep writing in it every day.

Here are other goals your coach (you!) could give you. Pick one a week, and one bigger one for a month. Write them down in your book.

▶ Take your notebook into a coffee bar, order your favourite latte and just write for 30 minutes to an hour. Look at what's going on; people-watch, but not critically – don't judge, just describe.

▶ Spend one evening looking through the Arvon course leaflet (www.arvonfoundation.org). You might be able to afford a course, you might not (they do have bursaries, just apply) – but just seeing what's on offer can trigger ideas.

▶ Check with your local Borders or Waterstone's bookstore to see which authors are visiting to give talks in the next month. Either free or around £3 (which is deducted from any purchase), they are exceptionally good value; sometimes they throw in a glass of wine. You can ask the author questions on your writing. It's as good as an expensive writing workshop.

▶ Plot an outline for an article contest advertised in *Writers' News* or *Mslexia*, or even the magazine article contest in this book. Just do the outline for now – the article itself will be your next goal or two.

▶ If you're at work, spend a lunchtime walking around a part of the city or town you never go to. Write a few notes on your impressions. These could form the basis for a magazine article.

▶ Send one piece you have written to an editor. If it's not wanted, send it off to another magazine – have envelopes and stamps ready.

▶ Take a short, manageable course – or begin a correspondence course – in creative writing, a foreign language, Thai cookery, or any subject that appeals to you. I know of no better way to begin to come 'alive' if you've been feeling jaded and heavy. If you want to learn a foreign language, try the *Hodder One-Day* CDs (www.teachyourself.co.uk). I learned the basics of Greek in one day! Make notes about it, enjoy it… then write about it!

▶ Prepare one short reader's letter for a magazine.

▶ Make preliminary notes for an opinion piece you want to write for a local magazine.

▶ Spend a half-day or even a couple of free hours researching a topic – it could be anything from the statues in your town to investigating two local attractions (an art gallery or museum? a park?) that you've never visited before.

▶ Buy a second hand book that interests you, and that could help your writing.

▶ Think about a travel writing article you could do, and perhaps begin to plan the trip today. Go to travel agents and pick up brochures.

I think, therefore I coach

Negative thinking produces negative results, but when you consciously put your writing aims down in black and white, your subconscious can do nothing other than respond positively. It's true that there are times when coaching yourself can be a struggle. Today, it took me an hour or two to get to my computer. I thought I didn't want to write – it was what I did all week, all the time. Give me a break! But ten minutes in, my commitment paid off and I was enjoying it. All thanks to my personal coach – me!

Now it's your turn! Get those writing goals down on paper and look forward to marching down that list, ticking them off. Reward yourself when you do.

Show the flag!

Starting to flag? Everyone wilts now and then. We all falter from time to time. Have a look at my coaching tips for when your writing – and maybe your life – isn't going too well:

▶ **THINK** strong, not weak. Don't think, 'It's hopeless, I'm too tired. It's too hard'. Replace this with, 'I'm strong and I write well. I can do it'.

▶ **BE GLAD** you've got this weekend just to write – and to live.

▶ **IF** you feel tense, rest on a sofa and let your body relax for a few minutes; listen to a short relaxation tape or soothing music. Then go back to the computer until it's time to stop!

▶ **TAKE** a few minutes to tidy your workspace, so it will be fresh for you – you can do this at any time.

▶ **PLAY** music that uplifts you.

▶ **DON'T** aim to be perfect, just productive. Above all… write.

Dodging the demons

Depression, fatigue and disappointment can clobber your resolve. Many writers suffer from occasional bouts of mild depression which plays havoc with their work. If you have a demanding, full-time job, it may be that you can just about manage during the week, but slump into the weekend feeling tired, flat and drained of energy. You can't even think about writing.

It may be that disappointment and rejection has got you down. It could be to do with your writing or with something else – but whatever it is may drain your vitality and your energy for writing.

There are things you can do to help yourself. To tackle these demons, we need to let go of the 'stand and deliver' attitude to life – the attitude that insists 'I must never be annoyed by anyone… insulted… rejected… treated badly'. The list goes on; my own 'must never' list can read, on a bad day, like a phone directory!

That 'stand and deliver' challenge to life was often instilled by parents who were overly protective in ensuring that their children were never subjected to insults, rejection and bad treatment.

They wanted only the best for their children, but this can work against you as a writer. Rejection is an unavoidable part of the writing package – you have to be able to handle it. If you're too crushed or angered by it, if 'stand and deliver' is too ingrained in you, you'll never submit or even finish magazine features; you'll be expecting magazine editors to be ringing you with choice commissions!

If you spend too much time seething over imagined or real insults, you'll never get around to writing! You'll never feel like it, you'll be too fed up and angry.

You can replace the 'musts' with more rational thinking. 'I must not be rejected ever' could be replaced with, 'I would much prefer not to be rejected, but I can take it if I am, because there are no guarantees in life!'

Use self -reaffirmation more often and consciously:

'I tried my best with my article; being rejected does not mean I am no good.'

'My style did not match their requirements or preferences this time. Yes, I'd prefer not to have the piece rejected, but I can take it!'

Sleeping lion

Lack of sleep – with troubled minds kept awake by tumbling thoughts and worries – can be another obstacle to writing. Here's the advice from my friend, Dr Milind Jani:

"The secret of good sleep lies in balancing the activity during the day and doing meditation with relaxing music, exercise and deep breathing in the evening."

So – add a little exercise to your hours spent at the computer! Even a brisk half-hour walk around the block will help you sleep later on. Then in the evening, try a relaxation tape; *Nine Ways To Touch The Soul* (www.momtazi. com) includes the soothing sounds of the sea.

I recommend a glass of warm milk with Milind Jani's almonds and nutmeg mix (Peaceful sleep mixture – www.pavilionhealth.co.uk), or try a fortifier such as his Energy Plus… you take a spoonful or two daily for energy and prevention of infections.

If you're lying awake with a churning mind, it's better to get up and make notes in your coaching diary. List the problems and write down some 'automatic' thoughts about them. Write through the problem. It's possible that these personal notes will later form the basis of an interesting magazine article… perhaps about you and sleep!

Top tip

Write a few lines to yourself every day in your coaching notebook.

Desert Island Books: Eight top books to help you

Writing Down The Bones, Natalie Goldberg (Shambhala, £10.99)

Write It Down, Make It Happen, Henriette Anne Klauser (Simon and Schuster, £10)

Writing a Novel, John Braine (Eyre Methuen – look in second hand shops)

Bestseller, Celia Brayfield (4th Estate, £7.99)

Manage Yourself, Manage Your Life, Ian McDermott and Ian Shircore (Piatkus, £9.99)

Becoming a Writer, Dorothea Brande (MacMillan, £9.99)

You Can Have What You Want, Michael Neill (Hay House £9.99)

Change Your Life in 7 Days, Paul McKenna (Bantam Press £8.99)

Focus! Focus! Focus!

Maybe your demons aren't stress, depression or sleeplessness, but just a problem concentrating. You may – probably will – have a problem staying focussed this weekend. Don't worry. You wouldn't be human if this didn't happen! Even if you were on a residential weekend course, your mind would wander sometimes; you'd be looking out of the window, thinking about a swim in the hotel's pool, looking forward to dinner – or wishing you were somewhere else.

Why do we have such trouble concentrating? Part of the difficulty is that we pay far too much attention to incidental and unimportant messages from the brain. For example, if you are trying to write an article and you suddenly think, 'We're out of bread! I must get some', or, 'I forgot to put the washing machine on', the temptation is to get up and do something instantly about your 'urgent' brain messages.

But these annoying messages can be ignored. Focus only on your writing. Do the errands when you would normally do them, and wait for a natural break to switch the washing on. Make lists of essential chores and do them all before you begin to write. When new messages pop out of your brain, just let them pass by. If you were in an office, you couldn't do anything about them anyway: your washing machine isn't there, and colleagues might not understand why you've left an important meeting to buy bread. So, behave the same way when writing at home this weekend.

We need to control our mind, not let it control us. It takes practice and discipline, but it pays off.

Re-energize – 7 tips for the next 7 days

- ▶ **BUY** a copy of Paul McKenna's *Change Your Life In 7 days*. (Bantam Press, £8 99) this week. The book includes a CD, which can't fail to improve your mood.

- ▶ **IN** the morning, switch your computer on before you have a cup of tea, coffee or breakfast. When you sit down to work, it's waiting for you – it helps.

- ▶ **KEEP** your writing space extremely neat. The more clutter there is, the more your brain has to grapple with. Keep a Zen-like order and you'll be surprised how much better you'll work.

- ▶ **HAVE** business cards printed – you can get them done free this weekend at www.vistaprint.co.uk. In a few days, you'll have your own cards with your name and the words 'magazine writer' on them.

- ▶ **WALK** around a part of your town or city that you'd normally avoid. A short walk is fine. Look at the houses, shops the people; note the spirit of the place; listen to what people say… you'll be surprised and inspired.

- ▶ **BUY** *The Big Issue* and talk to the vendor for a few minutes.

- ▶ **MAKE** a to-do list at the end of your writing day, just as you would in an office.

Vital tips

Vital tip 1 – Be your own best friend. Don't beat yourself up for not writing or writing something you think is nonsense. Stay with it, and you will find you can improve it.

Vital tip 2 – Discipline! You know you have writing you want to do. You also know you will feel disappointed with yourself if you don't do it. And you know, too, that disappointment can lead to depression. Avoid the angst – by doing what you want to do anyway!

Picture this!

Finally, I want you to leave this session with a clear vision of your writing success. You'll need to stretch out on a sofa or on the floor. You'll need to close your eyes.

Here's a visualisation I've used many times. My much-loved personal coach, Michael, gave it to me. You can use it too.

► **BREATHE** deeply

► **VISUALISE** your name in a magazine in WH Smith's

► **MAKE** the image huge, coloured and full of vitality – like a movie

► **SEE** your smiling face as you open the magazine

► **SEE** the racks of copies – all with your name inside them!

► **HEAR** your friends and family congratulate you!

► **SEE** your happy face – look into your smiling face – keep that vision before you all day

6 – The practicals

'The ability to express oneself in clear, correct English is an accomplishment, like being able to play the piano. Not everyone can do it well, but for sure everyone can learn how not to do it badly.'

~ Keith Waterhouse, *English Our English (And How To Sing It)*

Now it's time to look at the bare bones of writing technique – all the practical how-to you need to create good magazine articles. For this chapter, you don't need to do anything; just read and absorb. Taking a few notes is helpful, or put yellow Post-Its on pages you think you might want to go back to. You will probably want to get advice from it over and over again – this is your 'workbook' reference section.

Sit back on the sofa, or even out in the garden if it's warm enough. This is a section to read and digest, but don't expect to remember all of it immediately. And don't be put off by seeing how much there is to learn. You will find you pick up certain things quickly and remember them. You might have to check on other techniques several times before they stick. Don't worry – as long as you have this practical guide, and you use it, you won't go wrong.

Sound writing technique is vital, but never forget it's the ideas you have and the vitality of your writing that will make it irresistible to editors. And this weekend you're creating articles just from your ideas – you've dedicated this time. You are investing in your own creativity. But the more professional your work is, the better your chances of success.

In this chapter, I'm going to give you all the basic techniques you need for the polishing and finishing that's essential before submitting work to editors. From my experience as a writers' Agony Aunt, it's not the basic ideas or the writing itself that handicaps new writers: it's just that they're not motivated to finish and polish their work. They worry about the structure until they become so anxious that eventually their piece remains unfinished. They believe that their work has to be 'absolutely perfect' and 'much better' before they send it away. But what is 'perfect'? You can go on and on re-working your articles. But this is counter-productive. You become confused and doubtful and even tired of looking at your own words.

Often the problem with finishing articles is a confidence thing. Maybe in the past you showed your writing to a partner or friend and they didn't quite 'get' it? Or perhaps they criticised it, denting your pride in it and lowering your resolve? Maybe they offered too many suggestions, helping you to lose faith in your own ideas. Perhaps you've even had a rejection letter, and didn't like its tone? This has happened to all writers. It's happened to me more than once! But it won't happen this weekend! You may have already drafted a couple of pieces, but with these practical tips, you can finish and polish them. You can groom your writing for success.

Reporter!

How did I acquire the essential techniques? I didn't go to university. When I left school at 16 and joined a local newspaper as a junior reporter, I was taught practical tips in my first few weeks. Since I already loved English and enjoyed writing – and I'm assuming you're the same, or you wouldn't be reading this book – it didn't take me long to pick them up.

One of the first things I learned was that there was no better verb than 'said' for reported speech. It's better than declaimed, announced, uttered and retorted. I also learned to write the introduction – the first paragraph – to an article last; there are times when you need to have written the body of an article before you can find the best way to introduce it. I learned rapidly to: keep paragraphs short; include a whole idea in each paragraph; avoid clichés – avoid them like the plague! – and slogans; to cut through pomposity and wordiness; and to cultivate a mania for fact-checking.

These principles of writing remain absolutely unchanged. Computers, e-mail, the internet, how-to-write software – these have altered nothing about the basics of good feature writing. That's why my practical training as a journalist, pre-computers, has kept me constantly in interesting and occasionally well-paid work for a career spanning decades… despite seismic changes in technology. Despite the fact that technology isn't my strongest point, I've been lucky enough to hang on to good jobs when younger writers with a thorough knowledge of and profound interest in computers have lost theirs. So, grasp these basics and combine them with your own talent and ideas. You don't need an MA in Creative Writing, a doctorate in Media Studies or a sheaf of word processing certificates. All you need is you!

Tips from a reporter's office

I started work straight from school in the years before computers. On my desk at the newspaper office was a spike (literally a metal spike on a wooden stand) to 'file' all used bits of paper – cuttings, press releases, notes. Over the year, the spike became crammed with hundreds of bits of paper that couldn't get lost. Crude? Yes, but it meant information you might need again could always be found. You can do the same with your computer – file and keep copies of everything you write, updating each version with a number. For example, `statelyhomewilts1`, `statelyhomewilts2`, and so on. Updating each version with a simple number means you will never find yourself working on – or worse still, sending out – an old version. Sadly – and unlike the good old spike, which never broke down – a computer can implode and lose all your work and notes. So save it onto a CD or floppy disc too – then it should, fingers crossed, be safe.

Ever scrabbled around looking for a bit of paper with a vital phone number scribbled on it? A number you need for your writing? You don't want to do this – it wastes time and it fills your head with uninspiring anxiety. Always keep cuttings and useful notes in polythene folders labelled with the article's working title and the date you start the work. Here's another way if you're folder-phobic… buy a scrapbook and tubes of paper paste, and simply stick in all those scraps of notes and leaflets containing vital info.

My first purchase as a reporter, though, was a 'contacts' book – just a chunky, sturdy address book in which I wrote down the contact details of everyone I talked to in the course of my work. You can do this, or keep a computer database, with e-mail, website and postal addresses, and phone numbers. Over the year, you build up an excellent network in your contacts book. If you buy the same kind of address book when that's filled, you'll collect a personal reference library that will be helpful again and again.

Keep things tidy! Every three months at the newspaper we were encouraged by the chief reporter to clear out and even polish our desks. I admit I didn't always do it – my clear-out was more like once a year – but there's no doubt that a tidy desk helps when you are writing. Losing things – notes, essential leaflets, pictures, stamps – all adds up to stress and time wasted.

My early start

When I left school at the age of 16, I started almost immediately to write articles that would be read by 20,000 readers every week.

Looking back, it seems an enormous task for the weekly newspaper I joined: to teach me, a schoolgirl, how to write for a publication that everyone in this West Country town read. It was their news bible! The newspaper had a total editorial staff of five – the editor, a sub editor, chief reporter and two apprentice reporters, one of whom was me.

In the second week I was there, the chief reporter asked me if I wanted to take over the Woman's Page. I could write about anything I liked, and interview anyone who'd agree to be interviewed by me – and my photograph would be on the page! I could not conceal the thrill this gave me, even though I knew I would be working on it in what was left of my own time, since the week was taken up with covering cases at the local magistrates court, reporting town council meetings, going out on news stories, writing obituaries and even compiling tide timetables – this was a seaside newspaper.

But writing this page meant my skills were fast-tracked – the chief sub-editor, who'd worked for years in Fleet Street, gave me a personal copy clinic on my page every week. This kind of one-to-one tuition from an award-winning professional would today be worth several thousand pounds. Bert was semi-retired and worked three days a week on the newspaper. He coached me in his own time, although journalists make no distinction between 'my' time and 'office' time; it can't be a 9-to-five job. My parents complained that they never saw me, and why didn't I take my bed to the office? Their other complaint was that I never had time to tell them the news, even though I worked at the very hub of it – they had to wait for the newspaper to come out!

The editor was a shadowy figure who kept to his room – with only his enormous dog for company. He rarely spoke to me except to interview me for the job, and once to give me one piece of excellent advice:

"When you interview someone famous, always ask them what they had for breakfast. Get the detail."

This was long before *Hello!* was invented, and of course he was right. It was one of the best pieces of writing advice I ever had. Adding detail has always worked in my articles, and will in yours. But this silent editor was a worker. He could be seen, wearing an inky printer's overall, working tight-lipped on pages in the furnace-like basement where the hot metal printing press was. On Thursday evenings, until late into the night, it churned out thousands of newspapers. I loved to see the papers come out, particularly 'my' women's page, which was called Coffee Break. I interviewed local models and beauty queens, old-time cookery gurus like Fanny Craddock, visiting celebs such as Veronica Lake, Acker Bilk and Helen Shapiro, and pop stars who'd found Jesus while in re-hab. With most articles, I included boxes of tips: do's and don'ts for how to make lipstick stay on, and how to cook the perfect Christmas dinner... these topics don't seem to have changed. I would interview, say, three local people about how they would spend Christmas Day: one would be a mother of five, one a pensioner living in a bedsitter, one a bachelor priest. They'd tell me their timetable for the day, their food hints and tips, how much they'd spend, what they might have to drink and how they really felt about Christmas. Even at 16, I'd grasped what it is that readers want: detail, detail, detail!

It was the personal coaching and the goal-setting inspired by Bert that rapidly improved my writing. When he suggested that articles I wrote could be sent to the women's page of *The Daily Telegraph*, his belief in me meant I never doubted that I'd succeed.

Top techniques

Lots of the techniques are simply common sense. For example, each time you write an article, draft out a 'plot' – with a running order – first. The plot is the story of your article, with a beginning, middle and end. Introduce your ideas in a 'hierarchy' – with the most arresting or original fact or idea first, then the others in descending order of significance. It's the way you'd tell a friend about something that's happened – with the most dramatic fact first, followed by the other bits of information in diminishing order of importance.

At the bottom of each page of hard copy (that's old-fashioned paper, not text on a computer screen), put 'mf' (more following), and at the bottom of the final page, the word 'ends'. That way, it's crystal clear when there's more to come, and when the piece is finished.

On the top of each page on the right, put your surname, e-mail address and phone number – that's all. That way, on every page, your contact details are clear. And if a sheet of paper gets detached, it's easy for the editor to know where it comes from.

When you e-mail your work, send it as a plain Word document attachment. Your work should be neatly arranged in paragraphs, but you don't need to format it in any way. Don't ever be tempted to use colours, highlights, boxes or borders. No formats and fancy fonts! Keep things totally simple.

Never send to magazines original documents and photographs, especially if they're not yours; publications aren't responsible if they're lost or damaged. Send your feature on paper – that's hard copy – but always offer to send it on a disc or by e-mail if your work is accepted. File everything on your computer in folders marked with the name of the magazine you are approaching, and also on a CD or floppy disc.

Top tip

Most magazines want your features submitted on paper, neatly organized along the lines I've outlined. They don't want their e-mail in-box clogged up with submissions; they want to be able to read your work on paper. Once you become a regular, you may be asked to send in work sight unseen by e-mail. But magazine features are always printed and read on paper. This has not changed in the computer age.

Simple subbing

One of the very first things I learned was that after a feature has been written, it must be 'subbed', or sub-edited. It's a checking and revision process that ensures the article is fit for publication. Magazines and newspapers used to employ large teams of sub-editors who would check your work for you. Increasingly, this layer of professionals has been reduced – writers are expected to handle the basic subbing themselves. There may be one multi-skilled sub who can do a little work on your article, but the less there is for him or her to do, the better. Editors will favour freelance writers whose work requires minimum revision.

These are the aims of subbing:

▶ To make your feature fit the number of words required – read articles in the magazine you aim at and count the number of words in the published features. Then ensure your feature is not longer or very much shorter. There's no point in sending a 10,000-word feature to a magazine that never runs anything longer than 2,500.

▶ To ensure that everything that can be checked has been checked – phone numbers, websites, dates, name spellings and statistics.

▶ To ensure that there's nothing in the article that is a potential libel, or offensive.

Sub these out!

Subbing can sometimes entail adding material – words, sentences or whole paragraphs, and it can often mean cutting copy. Don't use any of these:

▶ Swear words

▶ Slang words or jargon

▶ Official-ese – English as used by politicians, civil servants and estate agents

▶ Words, even written jokingly, that would be hurtful or offensive to minority groups

▶ Words that could damage someone's reputation

Your crash course in subbing

Subbing was traditionally done in red ink, so printers could quickly identify the corrections. To this day, subbing corrections are marked in red on the hard copy. You'll have equipped yourself with a few red pens this weekend, so you can do it the professional way, on your own work!

Obviously, subbing on screen is much quicker, and you can use the timesaving wordcount. But do not rely on your computer's spelling and punctuation checkers. These can be an unreliable guide through the quagmires of the English – and American! – language. So write and first sub your article on screen, print it out, read it again, make further the corrections in red and then amend on screen. You will be looking for:

▶ spelling mistakes

▶ adjectives, nouns and verbs that you have repeated in the same sentence or paragraph

▶ punctuation errors

▶ over-long sentences

▶ mixed-up tenses

▶ verb confusion

Print out and check again. Keep doing this until there are no red marks.

Do not expect to sub (or copy edit, as the Americans call it) your article to perfection in one go – I will do three or four subbings before I'm convinced an article is as perfect as I can get it. But when you've done all you can – yes, send it out!

Avoid getting too many opinions from family and friends on your work. My view is that the more people you include for opinions on anything, the worse it gets! Some things can't be done by committee, and writing is certainly one of them. That's why this weekend course is ideal – you won't be surrounded by people making 'helpful' suggestions.

Clean copy

▶ Aim for succinct, 'clean' copy free of unnecessary adjectives and useless words such as *however, actually, personally, notwithstanding.*

▶ Keep it brief! The more economic you make each piece, the more gracefully it will read. Most copy can be cut by a third without losing any charm or information. Make every word work hard – and never use ten words when five will do the job. Plain English is what you're aiming for – not flowery prose. Cut out any signs of snobbery, pomposity or boasting in your own copy.

▶ Whether you're doing a 1,000-word piece, a reader's letter, or a 100-word tip, check everything thoroughly. Use reference books. Use a dictionary to confirm spellings – do not ask anyone; they could be wrong. Be accurate, always.

▶ Remember to answer all of the questions readers will be asking themselves: who, what, where, when, why and how? Don't leave readers confused.

▶ Make your first paragraph as sharp as possible – again, just write as you might speak. In any feature, the first fact that springs out in your mind is the one to begin with in your feature.

▶ You don't have to keep thinking of ways to say 'said' – there are few better words for this purpose.

▶ Got a long report you want to condense and tackle in your feature? Break it up by using 'bullet points' – digestible pieces of information distinguished by an asterisk or other mark.

▶ Don't expect readers to guess at titles of organizations. Whenever you use initials, always spell out the full title the first time you use it. So the NUJ is National Union of Journalists; the EU, the European Union; the PCC, the Press Complaints Commission, and so on. There are exceptions – the BBC and NATO are two – but there aren't very many. If you don't know what a set of initials stands for, you can't expect readers to know.

▶ Quotes from the *Bible*, Shakespeare and so on must be accurate. Editors won't use your features again if you get them wrong! Geographical references must be right, with locations spelt correctly. Political references must be absolutely current; don't rely on old cuttings or the internet.

▶ Use proper reference books.

Top tip:

The golden rule is: **If in doubt, leave it out!**

Plain English

Use plain English: nothing is more elegant. Pepper your pieces with words that fudge meaning, or with pompous or pretentious language, and your article will soon find its way to the editor's bin.

Here's an example:

Currently (Now)

At the present time: (Now)

In present circumstances: (Now)

At this moment in time: (Now)

Here and now: (Now)

On this occasion: (Now)

At this moment: (Now)

And here are some more…

Parking area: (Car park)

Kitchen area: (Kitchen)

Garden facilities: (Garden)

Garage area: (Garage)

Also avoid using clichés in your work. Clichés are phrases such as 'last but not least', 'I hear you say' or 'watch this space'. Modern clichés and slogans include phrases such as 'go for it' or 'bring it on' or 'off the radar'.

More clichés to avoid are:

Quality time

Short and sweet

Factor x

Hidden agenda

In the loop

Off-message.

Bit of a do

Pear-shaped

Neat writing tips

Knock one sentence into two short ones for your introduction to a magazine article. In most cases, the improvement will be 100 per cent.

Don't use foreign phrases or words – even in travel articles – when there are perfectly formed English – or sometimes American – words that will do the job. There is no place for frequent bits of French or Italian – please, no *mama mia!*, *au contraire*, *monsieur*, *madame*, *le patron* or *garçon*.

Beware of product trademarks – perfume rather than Chanel; mac or rain-coat rather than Burberry. But when you do have to use a trademark, it should begin with a capital letter.

Never rely on a computer to produce readability for you. Computers do clever things, but they don't have brains. Many of the 'corrections' a computer creates, in spellchecker or grammar tools, are incorrect. When I wrote this chapter, my computer tried to: change 'your' to 'you're' several times;

put commas in the wrong place; and changed correct spellings to incorrect ones. Computers have their place, but not where excellent English is concerned.

10 top tips

1 **RING** any phone numbers you've included, check e-mail and website addresses. Do not just assume they're right because they were in a cutting or leaflet – they may have been keyed in wrongly.

2 **ASK** people you interview to spell out his or her name. Even a simple name that sounds like Leslie, Lynne or Chris can be spelt in several ways. Is it John or Jon? Sarah or Sara? Lisa or Liza? It does matter, because people get annoyed when their names are spelt wrongly. Check. The worst thing is to have Lyn and Lynne when you are writing about the same person.

3 **CHECK** street spellings on a local map.

4 **CAREFULLY** check prices of everything you mention, whether it's a cheap ticket for a film, the price of a park 'n ride bus service or a supermarket sandwich. It may not seem that crucial to you – but the people involved can get upset if details go in wrongly. So can readers.

5 **INFORMATION** on a website can be reasonably usable, but will not compare with talking to an expert. Website information also goes out of date quickly, and was sometimes wrong to begin with. It's fine as a reference, but don't use it for material for an entire article.

6 **PRESS CUTTINGS** – especially about people – can be dangerous. You may find yourself repeating an inaccuracy or a libel, so be vigilant about what you use from old newspapers.

7 **WHEN** you quote from a book – or suggest it as a useful read – give the title, author and publisher.

8 **COPY** the style of the journal you are writing for.

9 **IF** you are using a quote from someone, it must be understandable. Don't pass on gobbledygook.

10 **IF** you use a quote from an article someone else has written about your subject or topic, attribute it to them: 'Louise Black, writing in *The Spectator* in 1989, said that...' Don't give the quote as if it were your own.

Libel at a glance

Libel – or defamation – law can be and often is very complicated and expensive, even before a case gets to court. In brief, a libel is the publication of a statement which exposes someone to contempt or hatred, which causes him to be shunned, or which could damage his or her livelihood. A libel is a statement, or an implication in a statement, that could blacken a reputation.

There are two main defences – and in most cases they are difficult and very costly to prove: that the statement is true (and the writer and publisher must be able to prove it's true – just believing it's true isn't good enough), and fair comment based on fact.

Now you're on your way to mastering all of the basic writing techniques, enabling you to become your magazine's favourite freelance. You will offer clean, query-free copy that will be gladly accepted by today's editors. It's worth learning some of the techniques by heart. This is the language of magazine article writing and you are starting to speak it!

7 – Travel on!

'…All you have to do is write one true sentence.
Write the truest sentence that you know.'

~ Ernest Hemingway, *A Moveable Feast*

Travel writing – is this one of your options for this weekend? I'm willing to bet it is – travel writing is the most popular strand in all of the college writing courses. And it's an option open to many more people than it used to be. Flight cancellations and delays apart, travel is so much easier and cheaper nowadays. We shoot off casually for weekends in Paris, or go on spur-of-the-moment breaks in Rome or Madrid – or just about every 'must see' city in Europe. We take creative writing holidays on Greek islands, paint in Provence, learn to cook Thai dishes in Bangkok and do yoga in Spain. We plan Christmas holidays in New York, autumn breaks in Venice and spring weeks in Sorrento. We take trips up the Nile and through the Amazon. And there's the big trips to Australia and South America and short hops to Amsterdam.

Travel offers instant pathways to excitement, change and refreshment. When you travel, you can almost be someone quite different. You can come alive, surrounded by new sights, re-acting to new experiences. And despite its affordability – and the ever-present risk of spending half of the first night or day of your holiday in an overcrowded airport lounge – travel has not lost its aura of special pleasure. It's still a thrill. And reading about a destination adds to that pleasure.

Home and away

You can write a travel piece from your desk this weekend – provided you have already made the trip! It could be about a resort – in Britain or abroad – you visited this year, a course you did in Barcelona or Brighton, a weekend trip to Paris or Prague, a city break in New York or Newcastle or a week in Santorini or Scarborough.

The first travel article I ever got paid for was published in a women's magazine. I was working in Newport, South Wales, and the magazine wanted a piece about Gwent. I didn't have to make the journey – I thought I knew every inch of it. Yet it took me for ever to finish the piece. After agonizing about what should and shouldn't be included, I ended up with a feature that would have been more at home in a travel company's brochure. The magazine's sub editors had to make several adjustments. They shortened my sentences, made it chattier and added sparkle. I know now what a travel piece needs: personality. All I need have done was describe the area, putting the emphasis on my favourite spots and listing my personal bests: shops, restaurants, interesting cafes, churches, parks, museums and so on. I could have found a 'landmark' date; an anniversary that would have given the feature a topical angle. I could have zoomed in on one particular aspect of Gwent rather than trying to cover the entire county.

It's a gift

The growth in the number of people who travel has been matched by the increase in the number of travel magazines. Look in WH Smith or Borders and you'll see the rows of travel mags lined up there. They all eat up copy every month; they all need freelance articles.

I edit a monthly glossy magazine about Greece (www.greecemagazine.co.uk). It's my job to select travel features for publication – and to find new, fresh writers. I launched an annual travel writing competition and every year the winners become regular writers for the magazine. I always look for the original, personal feature which informs and entertains. And here's the thing: I have built up a regular team of trusted writers, and not one of them is a trained, professional journalist. They are all very gifted amateurs who can write many qualified people off the page.

Think Shirley Valentine!

A travel feature need not be just a piece about an exotic holiday or a romantic city. It can be about a personal or emotional journey too – a post-divorce get-away on a Greek island, an exciting but doomed holiday fling in Rome, a re-union with a long-lost brother in Melbourne, or a colour piece about Berlin, perhaps, that threads in details about adjusting to a new job in a new country. What was it that made *Shirley Valentine* such a popular movie? It combined a love – or lust – story with a stunning Greek island setting.

Story line

Here are my three big tips for approaching the travel feature:

▶ Find an extra angle! Don't just write about the place, its history and geography. Yes, some of these aspects are necessary, but weave them in carefully and sparely. Don't cram it all in – you're writing an entertaining magazine feature, not a definitive encyclopaedia entry. If your trip is a landmark celebration – wedding anniversary, family re union, first trip with a baby – include how that went as well. There will be tensions as well as joys. Be honest. Talk about the downsides. Share more with the reader.

▶ Give your introduction a 'short story' quality! In other words, grab the reader's attention with an introduction that could just as easily open a short story. Begin with that "one true sentence".

▶ Zoom in on one incident, one situation, one event and give it more detail, more colour, more feeling. Explore just one train journey of a two-week rail holiday, one ferry trip from an island-hopping marathon. Take one aspect and open it up – again, like a short story.

The extra angle – and the 'short story' into – makes your feature irresistible. Here's how you do it.

Write your piece in the first person. Give your introduction a 'must read on' quality. You'll be giving it an onward momentum, a promise of something intriguing to come. Here are three examples of mine, which you can adapt:

1 *We bickered over whether to sunbathe on the vine-covered verandah, or wander down to the beach and swim in the sea. There were pros and cons. On the verandah, we'd be hammock-potatoes. Walking to the beach, we'd get hot and cross because there was no shade on the way. But at this beach there was a man dressed in waiter's white uniform, who came to your sunbed selling personal baskets of succulent fresh fruit. I've never seen that anywhere but Crete.*

2 *When we paid the lunch bill on the third day of our holiday in Sardinia, I saw my daughter smuggling a note into the young waiter's hand. He quickly concealed his shocked expression. She told us much later that it read "i don't even know your name! can we meet?" She was ten at the time. The rest of the holiday involved thinking of ways to console her. The drinks bill for us rapidly went above budget.*

3 *The marvellous thing about our hotel in central Naples was that on the top floor there were ornate luxury rooms with their own individual roof gardens. But they were surprisingly cheap – we could afford one each. We chatted briefly across the dividing*

wall, read our books and drank wine from a bottle of Prosecco we had sent up, balancing it on the balcony wall and being scrupulous about equal measures. Eight floors below us, Naples scurried about its business. Tourists straggled from the train station with backpacks and bags. We were really happy with our view of Naples and had no wish to leave our roof gardens and the peace of our luxury suites at the Hotel Cavos. We met for dinner only and occasional garden conversation.

No one would have guessed we were married.

With the 'must read on' quality, the 'short story intro', the rest of the feature becomes simple. You don't have to actually create a short story – it's just the introduction, to tempt the reader in and set the theme and tone.

Let's look at my examples above.

1 The theme for the Crete piece – on the island, it's possible for every taste to be satisfied. There's enough variety of scenery to please both the beach fan and the man or woman who likes to laze on a sunbed reading a book. It's the island with something for everyone.

2 There should be tips for other parents about dealing with pre-teen angst while on holiday. Ways of dealing with the pubescent daughter who falls in love with the waiter… it's pretty common and can cause holiday hell! Also suggestions on venues in Sardinia that will please both adults and older children. Reassurance that the reader isn't the only one struggling with family holiday headaches.

3 The final example – Naples – is an unusual take on how a couple can be as independent as they like while still enjoying each other's company. They're almost taking a holiday from each other – while still enjoying agreeable and familiar company when they have dinner! It's possible that many mature couples will warm to this one. There are practical suggestions for getting the most out of Naples – using its inexpensive luxury accommodation for a relaxing break, avoiding the crowds and backpackers but enjoying fine Italian dinners. Just because you're in a foreign city, you don't have to sightsee from dawn to dusk, getting tired and hot. You can pick and choose the elements you want to enjoy. You could use your roof garden as your personal open-air library for the week – why not?

Zoom in

By going deeper into one or two small incidents, you paint a more detailed and more colourful picture of your trip. You share more. These are two examples of mine from a piece I did on Athens for *Greece* magazine.

▶ *I drop into a crowded service at a Greek Orthodox Church. The priest is in full robes, the service scratchily broadcast to the people outside. A toddler lurches up to the altar with no one hauling him back. For an hour or more the priest sways and sings the service in a confident gravelly voice, acolytes sometimes planting kisses on his hand. The air is heavy with incense and emotion.*

▶ *I have dinner on the roof of the Hera Hotel. The charming staff serve me excellent roasted vegetables, stuffed tomatoes and tzatsiki with two glasses of white wine and mineral water. (The bill came to 36 euros and they threw in a glass of grappa.) A large party of Mid-West American retirees staying in the hotel have a group dinner with many exclamations about the "adorable" and "darling" floodlit view of the Acropolis ("will you look at that!") and much clicking of cameras. Soon the sound levels rise to a crescendo and the waiting staff are kept busy with more and more wine top-ups. Where would we all be without wine? Something to ponder on as I make notes and eavesdrop while upping my own alcohol intake – it's Greek and it's good.*

Take particular incidents on your travels and address them with more detail, closer observation, adding how they affected you as well. Eavesdrop. Zoom in.

Get personal

Offer readers particular experiences and original ideas. Be bold. By introducing feelings and personal situations, you give new travel ideas to your readers – ideas they may not have had and would welcome. Here's a good example from Jan Etherington, writing in *Good Housekeeping*:

Last year was a milestone for my three sisters   Teri, Di, Cheryl and me. The youngest, Cheryl, reached 50 and we realized we were all old enough to take a Saga holiday. That was our excuse for leaving husbands, children, grandchildren, and casseroles in the freezer and heading for the warm, green island of Madeira where we'd booked an oceanside hotel with a spa.

The rest of the piece talks not only about the spa holiday but also about how it brought the sisters closer. As they pamper themselves and reminisce, it's not only a good read but it also gives readers an idea – could they do the same with their sister? Combine travel with an idea like this and you might sell your piece, written three different ways, to three markets – for example, to a general women's magazine, to a spa magazine and, in addition, to a travel magazine about Portugal. For the women's magazine you'd be majoring on the sisters' holiday together, their relationship and how the holiday worked; for the spa magazine, the pampering and treatments; and for the Portugal magazine, the island of Madeira. There will be some elements in common – plus there will be the special angles for the three markets. Three different themes, but one lot of travel research on Portugal.

Win-win

Always write a travel piece with the intention of entering it later on for a writing competition. You have absolutely nothing to lose! File a paper copy, and a copy on your computer – then when you see an advertisement for a travel writing contest you've got something ready! It might need to be updated, but you'll have most of it ready.

I organize the judging of my annual travel writing competition for *Greece*, the monthly glossy magazine I edit. While the overall standard is very high, some of the entries, about a third, eliminate themselves on the first sifting. They fail because they:

▶ Cover too much in 1,200 words

▶ Are boring, plodding descriptions of a holiday

▶ Were lists of the good points only

▶ Began at the luggage carousel

▶ Read like a travel company brochure

▶ Lacked any sort of 'story'

▶ Used clichés for description

A possible winner can be spotted within the first few sentences. The feature engages you instantly because there's something there that tells you it will be different and honest, and that it will give the reader benefits. Here are a few examples of instant 'possibles'. They're similar to winning articles I have picked in my travel writing competitions.

1   *We'd been walking in Crete for two hours, and I was already sick of my walking companion's prattle.*

2   *My eardrums were blasted by a wall of sound. It was 2 a.m. and I was suddenly wide awake. The all-night disco on the other side of the olive grove had begun!*

3   *How many stuffed tomatoes can one person eat on one fortnight's holiday in Paxos? Too many, was my view. There was an alternative – stuffed peppers.*

These introductions herald intriguing features and leave the reader wanting more. They have my required 'short story' quality. The reader wants to know 'what happened next?'

1   On a walking holiday, how crucial is your companion's conversation? Is the writer joking, referring to his wife or girlfriend, or did he join a walking holiday with a group of strangers? We want to know, so we'll read on.

2   Was the all-night disco welcome to the writer or not? The exclamation mark suggests he or she was either ready to dance or have a nervous breakdown. We must read on to find out.

3   Apart from an excess of stuffed vegetables, what else did the writer like, or dislike, about Paxos? Some foodie detail is promised here.

The former *Northern Echo* editor and current editor of both *Holiday Villas* and *Holiday Cottages* travel magazines, David Kernek, says that when reading features sent to him by contributors, and judging travel writing contests, he has this very clear idea what he wants:

 "I look, at the very least, for a piece that's informative. It has to be written grammatically so that I can understand the information and I want it to convey something about the atmosphere and flavour of the destination. If I'm entertained by the writer's humour and get a sense of his or her personality, then that's a bonus."

His six tips are:

1   Write for your readers, who are looking for different places to visit. Look for different things to tell them about, if only briefly.

2   Keep your eyes open for the unusual. Your job is to notice things other people miss.

3   Be disciplined. You're providing an informative and practical overview, not a street-by-street, guidebook.

4   If you have a sense of humour, don't keep it out of your feature.

5   Spell place names correctly, and make sure your facts are right.

6   I find inconsistency maddening – for example, don't give some distances in miles and then swing into kilometres for others.

Ticket to ride

These are ten workable, typical ideas for travel writing. You could use them, or a version of them, to enter a travel writing competition:

▶ Cookery course based in Italy or France

▶ Wine-tasting holiday in the USA

▶ Holiday language course in Spain or Italy

▶ Out-of-season holiday on the edge of a lake

▶ Weekend break in New York or Berlin

▶ Singles holiday for older people

▶ Sharing a villa abroad with family or friends

▶ Creative writing holiday in Spain or Greece

▶ Holiday visiting a Wonder of the World, such as the Pyramids

▶ 'Retreat' holiday in a monastery – could be in the UK or abroad

Feel the food!

Travel and food and wine are closely linked. Mention of refreshments used to be just a 'comfort stop' in travel writing, but now it's considered essential. Readers crave descriptions of food and they need detail. So don't just write *"We stopped for a coffee"*. Write:

> *"We stopped in the main square in Athens, Syntagma, for a fragrant cappuccino topped with whipped cream and sprinkled with dark chocolate flakes – even the flakes were organic, according to the menu. But best of all were the miniature pastries, which accompanied our drinks. Tiny coffee eclairs, little strawberry tartlets and mini doughnuts lavishly dredged in icing sugar – each one just a mouthful. Syntagma is a bus terminal, tourist information centre and taxi rank all rolled into one. You couldn't enjoy more luxurious 'bus stop' refreshment anywhere in the world."*

Make jokes

You can use humour and irony – in fact humour is at a premium. Editors welcome it, provided their sense of humour matches yours. So do travel writing contest judges! When a judge is sifting 200-plus entries, something that makes him or her smile could be on the way to the first shortlist.

Here's a likely intro:

> *Day One of my cookery course in Rome and we're in the contessa's gleaming kitchen. Eight of us in the fresh white aprons embroidered with the name of her school. She gave us these aprons, indicating that we could buy them if we wished. Today we'll be doing a rich tomato and herb sauce with pasta, plus a super salad with an intricate dressing, plus tasting four 'matching' wines. It's taken me only ten minutes to realise that every other student knows far more about cooking than I do – they're all swapping clever insider tips. I thought this was a beginner's course!*

Cut the clichés

When describing a place, think of new ways to describe the obvious. Here are some very tired travel clichés and well-worn phrases that, to cite another cliché, should be avoided like the plague:

> *Pretty as a picture*
>
> *Pretty as a picture postcard*
>
> *Out of this world*
>
> *Living the dream*
>
> *Cloudless sky*
>
> *Clear blue sea*
>
> *Soft white sand*
>
> *Sparkling water*
>
> *Bustling café*
>
> *Sweet as honey*
>
> *Piping hot*
>
> *Steeped in history*
>
> *Full of character*
>
> *Quaint little houses*

Strive to find an original way to describe places. These are some of my favourite examples from *Greece* magazine. These writers took the trouble to avoid the overworn turn of phrase.

> *"The town folds down like a pac-a-mac during siesta"* (Crysse Morrison on Skyros)

> *"Ferries return the dead to the islands of their birth and supply the living with Coca Cola"* (David Kernek – Survival guide to island hopping)

> *"This villa is part of a pretty company of houses perched high on a hill"* (Kate Collyns, Glamorous villas)

> *"Shirley Valentine, whose story was filmed on Mykonos, stayed only as long as she did because a Greek waiter was keeping her in souvlakis"* (David Kernek, Five perfect islands)

> *"For some people, 48 hours in Athens is 47 too many. Give it a chance – it's Europe's most compelling capital"* (David Kernek – 48 hours in Athens)

Write local

If you're writing a local travel article, select something different and alternative. This doesn't mean the hippy trail! It means writing about your own town, city or neighbourhood but avoiding the conventional tourist destinations. For example:

▶ Docks areas – often redeveloped.

▶ Unusual churches and chapels – Bristol has an Eskimo church, for example. Most cities have one or two quirky churches.

▶ Cheap or even free refreshments – Bath City Art Gallery has a coffee machine where you make your own drink for a few pence.

▶ Well-hidden statues, shrines, gardens, parks and cafes which you, as a resident, know well – but which a visitor would be delighted to see.

▶ Private roof gardens, terraces, waterfalls and lakes which are sometimes open to the public.

Top travel market tips

▶ Activity breaks will be a good bet. Cookery, painting, walking or fitness holidays, perhaps written as a diary, from a first person point of view. Point out any downsides as well as all the plus points. For example: "Felt shy on the first day and began to wish I hadn't come on this holiday on my own. By the end of the evening, though, I'd got chatting to a couple of others who were also travelling solo. Tip: don't expect people to start chatting instantly, and at first talk more about the hobby – painting – than you do about yourself".

▶ Never forget the pulling power of the list. Can you come up with five perfect islands, ten places to stay, and eight great cafes in a city or resort? You may not need more than a listing (that's a phone number and prices) and a couple of lines about them.

▶ Travel differently – not just by plane. Did you do a trip by rail or sea that's normally done by air? This would make a good read. Many holidaymakers dislike flying and would be interested to see how feasible and pleasant a rail or sea journey can be.

▶ Did you do a holiday on the cheap – costs pruned to the bone – or, if you are being treated, in deluxe style? Why not write about your silver wedding in Venice, or your £15 a day island-hopping trip? Are you a vegetarian or do you have some other dietary need that must be accommodated on your holiday? You won't be the only one. Try a piece of travel writing that gives plenty of advice.

▶ Detail, detail, detail – I can't count the number of writers I have to chase on this… and pieces I have to reject because they lack detail, even though the idea was good. I noticed and noted down every detail of the meal we had at what might pass as a 'motorway' taverna in Crete, and every detail at the open-air cinema in Santorini – from the flowers in the ladies room to the colour of the seats. All you have to do is keep your eyes open and write things down.

▶ Food and wine are vitally important – in fact, if you can write about your cookery holiday in Greece, Thailand or Italy you're onto a winner. You can never write too much about food and wine.

▶ Use quotations from famous writers about travel, or fragments of appropriate poetry, at the start or end of your feature, but do so sparingly. Writing about Sardinia on an-out-of season holiday? Where the weather looks wonderful, but feels chilly? Try this quote from D.H. Lawrence, from *Sea and Sardinia* (1923): *"In the morning the sun was shining from a blue, blue sky, but the shadows were deadly cold and the sea like a flat blade of ice."* Get the quotes from *The Oxford Dictionary of Quotations*, or try the online quotation sites.

▶ Be honest; don't be tempted to gloss over grim experiences. "For travel pieces, I don't just want the good – I want the good and the bad," says Arline Usden of *The Lady*. "I want to know things about the place I could not find anywhere else."

▶ Keep your eyes open for the unusual. In Crete to do a travel feature, I noticed a wedding on the harbour at Chania. It made an extra, human touch.

▶ Balance your piece. Your nightmare resort might be paradise for somebody else.

▶ Think of a 'peg' – it might be a book or film that's just come out, or a landmark or anniversary celebration.

▶ Give readers a real feel of the place. Show, don't tell. The way it smells, the sounds you hear, the way things taste: even a dish as simple as chicken and chips will taste different abroad – describe it and record the extra herbs and flavourings.

More detail!

Readers crave detail. Here's four ways to get more in:

1 Remember that visual description is not the only way to create setting – notice sounds and smells as well. Use all the senses.

2 Look hard at your resort and find the colours that sum it up – in Greece, it's blue and white. In Venice, in December, I had an impression of navy blue – the canals – and parchment and gold for the stone of the buildings.

3 Snatches of dialogue can strengthen the sense of travelling in a different culture. But never lampoon the way foreigners speak English. How good is your Greek or Czech?

4 How about the modern culture of the destination? In Seville, I noticed the high grooming and polish of the city's modern young women: every one of them looked like a model. In New York, I reported that huge, first-class bookshops, both new and second-hand, are everywhere. This is a city that loves to read. Use modern culture as well as history.

Top tips

▶ Pictures are necessary to go with travel pieces. They can be prints, digital or slides – it's the clarity that counts, not the technical sophistication. You must also provide information so that the sub-editors can write captions for the photos. They're not mind-readers. And you should include some photographs of you. Make copies so that you don't have to ask for them back.

▶ Never be without a notebook and plenty of pens when you make a trip. Write every day. Jot down small details – prices of coffee, music that's played, country etiquette and customs, as well as your own thoughts and impressions. Keep a folder of postcards, cards and leaflets.

And finally, one perfect piece

I found this article by Sharon Glew in *The Lady*, headlined Tibetan Heights. I rate it as an ideal example of a travel piece. It has the writer's personality; the 'short story' intro; zoom-in detail; colour; history; the landmark date; and the essential travel listings.

> *Mountains with the far-off texture of dusty elephant skins form the ramparts of this surreal amphitheatre of the heavens. That anything earthly should look down on us seems quite a feat, tottering breathlessly as we are at over 11,811 feet (3,600m) above sea level. At Sera Monastery, north of the ancient Tibetan capital of Lhasa, the monks are anything but breathless: their hearts and lungs and sinew are on fire with the heat of a 300-strong debate.*
>
> *In groups of three, four and five they are crammed into an open courtyard of the monastery. On the sidelines, tourists shuffle round with competing clicks and whirls of cameras: they make uneven time with the cacophony of monastic debaters whose arguments now seem to include a few whoops... is this really Buddhism?*
>
> *At around 3.30p.m. every day, the young monks gather to consolidate the morning's Buddhist teachings through the art of philosophical debate. The triumphant exclamation "tsa!" (I conclude this point with feeling) punctuates each point. Choking chalk dust rises as each monk stamps home his position. The courtyard is a crucible of vermilion passions dancing their fury like flames.*

Instead of trying to cover the entire history of Tibet in 900 words, she zooms in on the debate the young monks held at one monastery. Closely, she describes the passionate discussion, watched by baffled tourists – and then:

> *Without warning it is finished. The monks form a submissive horseshoe and sit facing an elderly abbot on a raised platform. I want to hear the stern man speak...but we are ushered out of the courtyard by government officials. "What will they speak about?" I ask our guide rather petulantly. He won't catch my eye...*
>
> *"To think less of the Dalai Lama and his teachings. To look more to the Party, the Motherland."*
>
> *He looks sad and afraid.*

Travel on!

Sharon skilfully weaves in a little of Tibet's troubled politics; under its Chinese rulers, it is still an offence to posses a photograph of the Dalai Lama. And she includes a listings panel with five ways to get to Tibet, with websites and prices. The article was published to coincide with World Tibet day, July 3.

Now you!

So – you've picked the place you want to write about!
You've decided which magazine you will target.
You've counted the words they use – could be from 900 to 1,200
You've found an 'extra' angle.
You'll write in the first person.
You've thought of a 'short story' intro.
You may have found a 'landmark' date.
You will 'zoom in'.
You will send a picture of yourself.
And you will add a panel of listings.

Yes, you will write a travel feature this weekend and send it off!

8 – Writing for women's magazines

'Readers don't tell you what they want. They speak of "interesting articles", "good recipes", "half an hour of happiness", but the terms are not defined. You don't give readers what they want, but what they enjoy.'

~ Women's magazine publishers quoted by
Cynthia L. White, study of women's magazines for
the Royal Commission on the Press, 1977

Writing for women's magazines – is that your dream? I hope so, because I'd love to see you making a start on achieving that goal this weekend.

As you might have noticed by now, women's magazines are very close to my heart. I've always loved them. I love their glossy feel, even the fragrance of the pages; I'm enchanted by the promise they contain, the offers, the human stories, the opinions. I've always thought that a couple of pounds or so was a very small price to pay for the pleasure they give.

Though I buy books and movies too, women's magazines are my true addiction. A woman's magazine is a purchase that spells complete pleasure for me, and I suspect for millions of others. When I've bought two, or even three magazines at once, and been able to save them up and not read them all on the same day, it's as though there's a special treat waiting for me.

Yes, like most of us, I've had some dark nights of the soul, yet none that weren't eased just a little bit, and sometimes a lot, by a couple of brand new magazines to lose myself in! Whenever I've bought a crisp new magazine my spirits have never failed to lift. Yours too?

My ambition when I joined a local newspaper, straight from school, was always to write for women's magazines. When I was offered the newspaper's Woman's Page, I seized it eagerly, giving the benefit of my just-out-of-school 16-year-old's wisdom and advice on fashion, food and even bringing up babies! Within a year I was selling features to *The Daily Telegraph* woman's page, which paid me the equivalent of a month's salary for just one article. And as I progressed to being an award-winning woman's editor of several provincial newspapers, and then to work as a feature writer on international women's magazines such as *Woman's Day* and *Prima*, I found that what readers wanted to read had not changed over the years.

They want to read what other women say. What other women write. They wanted to read about their own lives, their own hopes and fears, their families and children, the challenges they face, the miseries they endure, the frivolities they enjoy, the addictions they can't give up, the relationships they negotiate and their triumphs, minor and major.

Let's be honest

You can get into women's magazines with one quality – honesty. The willingness to commit to the printed page something from your own life will get you there. You need clarity to convey it, but you don't need to be a great writer. You just need to write as if you were talking to a good friend. It's not about superb writing. It's about honesty, a clear writing style and learning the tricks of the trade. That, and the willingness to be generous with facts from your own experience and history.

There's always room for the fresh and honest voice, for the reader who can write, for the writer who understands completely the 'soul' of the magazine she wants to sell work to. You don't have to be an expert in anything except your own life. If you can express opinions, convey emotions, press a little bit of yourself onto the page – you'll succeed. Not everyone can do it! But you can – or you wouldn't have bought this book.

Me and you

The simplest idea could make a feature. Let's take a look at this one.

Eve ran a piece by Miranda Levy. It was headlined, *Me-time in a bottle.* The extremely simple point of the feature was this: Many mums with small children look forward all day to their glass of wine in the evening.

That's it! That's all!

The strapline, or sub-heading, was: *Candle-lit baths – pah! Admit it, says Miranda Levy, what most of us need to wind down is a sip of that 7 o'clock saviour.*

It began:

> *'Click' goes the door as I creep out of the bedroom, leaving An-*
> *nabel, three and Jacob, 18 months, dreaming. In seconds, I'm*
> *half-way down the stairs – sometimes, I think I'm going to trip*
> *over the stairgate and break my neck. I make it to the kitchen,*
> *reach out for the bottle of wine that just happens to be there on*
> *the worktop, pour myself a glass and – aaah.*

> *That first sip is one to savour: after a day of nappies, it's a*
> *warm, grown-up taste that reminds me I'm a person in my own*
> *right. Immediately, I'm back enjoying long romantic lunches*
> *with my husband, and anything that diverts me from cork-re-*
> *moving is met with selective deafness.*

And this is the last paragraph of this light yet so carefully judged feature:

> *At times, it does cross my mind to fight my mini-addiction – to*
> *try to last a night without a glass of wine. But then, I ask my-*
> *self 'why?' I've given up so much already: the going-out, the ex-*
> *pensive holidays, the fitting into size 10 Joseph trousers. So in*
> *my household, this one little indulgence is going to stay. Come*
> *7p.m, there's nothing sweeter than a closed kitchen door and a*
> *warm glass of Merlot in the hand.*

Eve's self-proclaimed selling point is *'beautiful, useful, real'*, and this feature covers all of these values. It's a magazine aimed at young, stylish women, many of them mothers of young children, mothers who'll be taking a break from careers. The writer name-checks many of the 'labels' *Eve* readers will recognise – Joseph trousers, Merlot wine, expensive holidays now unafford-able, children called Annabel and Jacob. It could just as well have been Amy and Jack!

Remembering my own time as a mother of a small daughter, how easily I could recognize that hour of the day when the house switched from being a kindergarten to a home for grown-ups. My back-to-sanity signal too, just like hers, was that single glass of wine – even the sound of the cork being pulled was a kind of tranquilizer.

But back to Miranda:

> *I admit it: as the last minutes before bedtime tick away and the*
> *kids snuggle down in front of Cbeebies, I'm planning my nightly*
> *treat. Will it be a hearty glass of Rioja or a couple of inches of Chab-*
> *lis left over from Saturday's dinner party?*

The sub-text of the feature confirms that somehow, despite the regrets for slim Joseph trousers and the lavish holidays, Miranda is in fact very happy with her life, and with her adored children. She still gives dinner parties and buys expensive wines. She loves to be with her husband enjoying long, leisurely lunches. Her article is light-hearted yet genuine, and grabs the target reader instantly.

Worried that this kind of feature suggests alcohol addiction? The writer includes a neat '*Eve* readers are responsible mums' get-out clause:

> *Before you call social services, I must clarify that my friends and I are pale, pathetic imitations of alcoholics. Most nights I can barely manage two glasses before I'm asleep... at the back of my mind is the knowledge that should I throw caution to the wind, I will surely pay. Mums cannot lie low and nurse a hangover.*

Tone the tone

It helps to carefully 'deconstruct' the style and tone of a women's magazine – and to follow that tone and style, without copying any of the content. It sounds difficult to do, but it isn't. You will need to read more than one issue. If you are a subscriber, that's ideal.

Start by reading one piece over and over again. Is the style neutral, warm, gushing, breathless, full of exclamation marks or with a slightly serious air? Is there a definite 'voice' – cosy, bossy, glamorous, frivolous? What kind of woman is writing – what stage of life is she at, and what's her attitude to life?

What you write must have a point, and it has to fit in to the way the magazine sees its readers. Study several issues of your target magazine. If the tone is right for you as a reader, it's right for you as a writer. And, despite a frivolous or amusing varnish, you'll find that women's magazines are always responsible, with high standards of journalistic integrity – far higher than many daily newspapers!

Here's the start of a piece by Tammy Cohen, writing in *Woman & Home*:

> *What's the greatest fear you have in your marriage now that 'mid-life' isn't just something that applies to the perishables in your fridge? Go on, be honest. Is it that he'll suddenly start wearing black leather, buy that 900cc motorbike he's fantasized about and announce that he's going to give up his job and sell the house? Or is it that he won't?*
>
> *Is your real fear...that he'll stick to the tried and tested, the same old same old, only now with less ambition, less energy and a lot less hair?*
>
> *And where will that leave you?*

Later, she asks:

...what happened? How is it that, while you're shopping at the same stores as your daughter, he's started dressing like your father?

Her argument – that while middle-aged women seem to like looking good, staying youthful and having fun, men become couch potatoes – is well explored. There's a touch of humour, a pinch of anguish, and that inevitable poignancy that comes when you look back to the distant first days of a long marriage. You'll never have any doubt that this writer is sincere. Yet she concludes that there are gains as well as losses in a 20-year old relationship. This isn't divorce territory for her. She sums up:

...one night it was actually a relief to stay in with a bottle of decent wine and a pair of deeply unsexy but cosy pyjamas and – oh, all right, I'll admit it – my partner of 20 years. The beauty was, I knew the following night we'd be out engaging with the world, so I could really enjoy our TV dinner.

Her piece is so right for the *W&H* reader – intelligent, balanced, modest. She clearly expresses the universal need for more a little more adventure in her life – combined with security of course. Women – and men – have been trying to find this elusive combination for centuries. It's one of the fundamental dilemmas of all our lives!

For women's magazines, you need to lock in to the feelings and frailties which all women share. The more honest you are, the more your voice comes through. This is Elaine Kingett, writing in *Woman & Home*:

The tumbleweed rolls down the hall. The dog sleeps all day and the house waits, holding its breath – unsure of its new job description. I have four bedrooms, three floors, two bathrooms and me. At the age of 56, I am living alone for the first time in my life.

Elaine, widowed three years earlier and with three children having left home, talks frankly about the strangeness of living on her own.

I find the situation scary, but equally exciting. I too feel like I've left home. Now the kitchen bin takes almost a week to fill and the contents moulder rankly in the meantime...with no one at home now, I feel less like going out, and with a five foot six inch-wide bed and the best duvet in the house, I'm still hoping someone may eventually join me in it!

This is honesty that warms the reader. The detail – from the kitchen bin problem to the admission that she'd like someone to share her bed – all are conveyed with simplicity and sincerity.

Fancy a current affair?

What do you want to achieve with your women's magazine article? Is it:

▶ Reader identification – your audience to sigh 'yes, that's how it is for me too'

▶ Shock, surprise, curiosity – are you writing about something extraordinary?

▶ A greater understanding of a big news event packaged in a feature that will appeal to women?

▶ A sense of adventure – are you offering advice on new beginnings, fresh starts, escapes, re-invention?

▶ Healing – advice about beauty, health, relaxation, coping with illness or an accident?

▶ Practical solutions – features that illustrate how you can save money, do things faster, beat stress, look younger, de-clutter?

You don't have to write about home life. Can you write about current affairs and political topics too? Offering illumination about a national or international issue is something many women's magazine readers appreciate. They want to be well-informed – especially when it could affect their children, homes, health, food and work.

They don't want all their news wrapped up in a heavy style, or delivered by ponderous pundits on a television programme you can barely remember after it's over. When it's in print, it can be read, digested, read again and understood.

Here's Anna Moore, in *Red* magazine, asking the question – how many children is enough?

> *As I write, my two daughters aged four and five are at school. The house is peaceful, (relatively) tidy and I have until 3.30 p.m. to work or flick through the papers. It's what I dreamt of when my girls were in the newborn stage, the nappy stage, the dawdling-through-parks-unable-to-think-because-you've-been-up-half-the-night stage. The stage when you're deducting childcare from your earnings and wondering why you bother to work at all. So we've finally got there, and guess what? I'm eight months pregnant. In a few weeks I'll be back behind that pram in the park, exhausted, impatient, not to mention poor. We've had to swap our Renault Megane for a Peugeot Estate and in a couple of years we'll probably need a bigger house too.*

Anna goes on to point out that most women are choosing to have smaller families – leading to a declining population. She collects interesting statistics from various agencies showing that in some countries with dwindling birth rates, women are being paid well by governments to have a third child. In France, they pay £680 a month for a year. Anna links this in an original way to her own story – that despite all the logical reasons not to, she chose to have a third child. She is well aware of the personal advantages there'd be in stopping at two, but she wanted another baby. She writes:

> *Financially and rationally, it's an insane decision to have another baby – but when it comes to planning your family, how rational are we? Who writes down pros and cons, or draws up spreadsheets of income versus costs?*

Even in a fact-based article like this, the writer adds *Red*-type personal detail right down to choice of cars – from Renault Megane to Peugeot Estate. Her conclusion is that the lowered birth rate is *"overwhelmingly the outcome of women choosing for themselves whether and when to bear children...there could be no better reason."*

For her this choice means having a third child. Many women will identify with the 'emotional' choice that defies all the intellectual arguments. It's what women's magazines are all about!

This is Christina Roberts, in a piece headlined *The accidental ecologist* in *Easy Living:*

> *My New Year's resolutions are as follows: this year I will have more candlelit dinners and do less laundry. I will spend less time in my car; more time walking and I will cook healthy delicious food from the best seasonal ingredients. If you join me, we will not only be happier and healthier; we will also be leaders in the battle against global warning.*

She goes on to talk about energy savings she could make: using her machines less, buying locally-grown food, walking for all short trips, car-sharing, turning down the heating thermostat. There's nothing new here (and there doesn't have to be – when you write magazine articles!) yet she's gone at it from a new angle:

> *When I checked, one third of the clothes in my dirty laundry basket were not actually dirty... if you live in a city, getting food delivered helps... an energy efficient lightbulb can save £60 of electricity over its lifetime. This is where my candlelit dinners come in.*

With features about current affairs, you can collect cuttings from newspapers and magazines about topics that interest you, then quote from them.

That's your research done, the rest is your opinion. My mantra is collect, cull and create! If you begin to do it this weekend, you'll be gathering information for future features with all your facts and figures to hand. And you don't need that many facts – nor do you need to analyze them yourself. Newspapers have already done all the work for you! They sum up all major research and reports in their own pages – on health, food, energy, population trends and education – all of which you can use for your own writing.

Date each cutting and collect them in folders. The statistics in research papers and government reports are open to anyone to quote from, for any kind of feature. They're yours for nothing – but make sure you attribute them in your feature. Think about basing an opinion or personal piece for women's magazine on them. You can get information from the internet too, but remember not all of it is edited and much of it is inaccurate. Anyone can post anything on it. I'd always go for news research in print. Remember – just one new thought on an old topic, and you're in.

Here's another feature opening, by Hazel Martin in *Woman & Home:*

> *My daughter grins like a loony as she skydives at 20,000 feet. Every time I watch the video, I panic as she steps off the plane into the cool blue air. It's the same panic I felt last year when I left my job, with redundancy pay as a financial cushion and no ties. I was free... but I felt directionless, alone and scared. I created a bubble of panic and got stuck in it.*

Tired of *"sleepless nights and anxious must-find-a-job days"*, Hazel dug out some old clothes and canvas and painted for a day.

> *"I started to relax. I stopped my frantic search for a job. I thought about working for myself."*

> She went on courses and *"once I'd stopped agonizing, my mind cleared. I was able to see a pinprick of light at the end of the tunnel. Now I know it's there, it's easy to focus on it – and it's getting bigger."*

Her feature gives useful advice about courses to go on, yet the great value of her writing is that it creates immediate empathy with the reader. These situations are universal. Who hasn't felt panic when they were out of work, and found themselves immobilized by it – unable to take steps forward?

Once again, it's honesty that wins in women's magazine writing. And what makes Hazel's different is the way she compares and links her feelings about losing her job with those she has when she sees the video of her daughter skydiving: panic. With this attention-grabbing introduction (known as an intro in the trade), she pulls readers in immediately.

Top tip

You can illustrate all of your women's features with case histories, personal stories, box-outs, contact numbers and addresses. Never forget the slogan: readers want news they can use. So don't write about a help group or association without giving its contact number, website or e-mail address. This is vital.

Topical tips

Topics vary in women's magazines, yet so often it's the small and simple things that count. Here's a perfect example. Women's magazines have been running features about sales for a hundred years at least. Just to show you how this hardy annual can always be re-angled, here is the intro to Maggie Alderson's *Easy Living* feature:

> *Here's something I hear way too often from friends.*
> *"I don't bother with sales, because I never get anything good."*
> *I have a very simple reply to that: are you mad?*

That's a new angle skillfully constructed. Most writers tell us to ignore the sales, because we'll waste money on things we don't want, but Maggie says:

> *In my opinion, the only way a woman with an income even slightly lower than Paris Hilton's can be anything like well dressed is to become a master sales shopper. Of course, you have to be a high-street wizard and a vintage queen too, but it's the stellar designer pieces picked up at sales over the years which are the backbone of my wardrobe. I love sales. They're such a game. You and your credit card pitted against the stores (not to mention other shoppers) and it is by taking just such a strategic sporting approach that you will get the really good gear.*

This piece has honesty and vitality. I also like the use of adjectives such as 'stellar', 'strategic' and 'sporting' – there's some careful phrasing here. She then adds a panel of tips – each with a nugget of clear information.

This is the perfect way to do a tip box, as she has done:

▶   Invest – Pay more than you normally would for a classic piece that you'll wear for years.

▶ Buy in multiples – if you find a really good cheap staple buy several – but only in classic colours.

▶ Think strategically – Not best money, but best value.

▶ Beware label frenzy – Don't buy something because it's your favourite designer and it's reduced. It does have to suit you too!

▶ Go crazy – Try on things you wouldn't if they were full price.

▶ Take risks – If it suits you but isn't your usual style, but it's ridiculously cheap – buy and sell on eBay later if it's no good.

▶ Work at it – rifle through every rail. You never know.

Tricks of the trade

Write as you would talk to a friend, making your conversation entertaining and sometimes amusing. Try these phrases in your articles:

You… yes you!
Oh, all right I'll admit it
Go on, be honest
And, you know what
Guess what?
See what I'm up against?
The beauty of it is
The devil you know
Go on then
If you say so
Not so bad
Yes and no
Give it a try
What's it worth?
Think about it

Use your friends!

It's useful to be able to quote a reader of the magazine you're writing for. If you have a friend who reads the magazine, she'll be an ideal case study. You can even begin your article by quoting her. If you use only her first name, there's no need to get her agreement. But if the topic is sensitive or controversial, change the name. These are three examples I've created:

1   *It wasn't until my friend Mary admitted that she never did any spring-cleaning – or much of any cleaning – that I realised we both hated housework. So how was it our homes are both fairly presentable?*

The answer was in the housework short cuts offered in Woman & Home *over the years. We're both addicts of the fast track, quick-fix 'instant' cleaning tip. We've even used the same hint for making a room seem just-cleaned – spray polish into the air. We've used that one over and over again. " I don't spring-clean, and thanks to* Woman & Home *I never have to!" was Mary's mantra.*

2   *Believe it or not, I had shared a dormitory during WW2 with a woman who lived four doors from me. It wasn't until we met in the newsagents – both of us buying* Woman *magazine – that we realized it. The magazine had an article about pen friends who'd kept writing though the war. "I still have a penfriend from my army days on the Isle of Wight," Sue said as we stood by magazine rack. We started swapping memories and before long discovered our link. Since then we've had coffee together many times. But it was* Woman, *which introduced us!*

3   *Every time I go to my friend Anna's for lunch, she cooks the same chicken casserole – from a* Good Housekeeping *recipe. Every time she comes to mine, I dish up my beef stew, also from good old GH. And we've been doing this for years. Neither of us can ever think of any new recipes! We always have a glass of wine with our meal, with Anna proposing " a toast to our chef GH!"*

'Fess up

Writing from home in this weekend, you can tackle personal articles or 'confession' pieces. This doesn't mean necessarily revealing the secrets of your sex life, or anything illegal or scandalous – just a personal experience you can share with other readers. It can mean confessing something uncomfortable, guilt-inducing, embarrassing, poignant, sad or frightening. It could be about health, parenting, your own childhood, work, school or money. It could be about sex. The more popular your style, the more you can reflect the lives of a middle-of-the-road readership, the more opportunities there are for you in writing for women's magazines.

Emotional and health-related confessions tend to be deeply personal There are key phrases that occur repeatedly in these sometimes very moving pieces:

> *All I ever wanted*
> *Or so it seemed*
> *One the outside, I was...on the inside...*
> *I tried so hard*
> *No one understood*
> *I may have seemed*
> *I couldn't go on*
> *I was two people*
> *I felt imprisoned*
> *I felt split in two*
> *I tried to escape*
> *I felt I was acting*

The key qualities for the writer of confession pieces – and relationship-based articles – are

▶ Sincerity

▶ Honesty

▶ Understanding

▶ Empathy

▶ Kindness

▶ Non-judgemental attitude

When you write your confession piece, write to the length of the one-page features within the magazine – usually about 750 to 850 words, depending on the size of the illustration, which could be a drawing or a photograph, used.

Here's an example I've created.

> *On the outside I was the perfect mother, always well dressed – clean jeans and a crisp shirt to meet my girls, Zoe (5) and Hayley (7), from school. I'd smile and greet other mums, listen to news about the PTA, contribute my home-made sausage rolls for the bring-and-buy. What they didn't know was that for a year I woke up every morning to daily inner terror and misery – I was facing a court case in which I'd be accused of stealing from my previous employer.*
>
> *That year was the longest of my life.*

You'd be writing a piece like this after the event has been resolved – but setting it as though you're still living it. You need to grab readers' attention with your feelings, the split between how things would seem to others and how they were to you. It could apply to anything crucial that has happened to you – illness, bereavement, money troubles, serious family problems, housing traumas. There will always be other readers who have been in the same situation. You're writing for them, as well as for yourself. And you can commit to paper emotions that, perhaps, you've never even told those closest to you.

Take a tip from Take A Break

The biggest-selling magazine in Britain today is *Take A Break*. It majors on its lively mix of true life stories, cookery, travel, health, fashion and beauty plus opportunities for readers to better themselves and their families.

The editor says the magazine is "a mirror of its readers lives and no-one else's. Our readers are women who find life tough but rewarding. They are sustained by family and relationships. Readers are in their 40s and largely working class. "We are anti-casinos, anti-smoking and anti-bad behaviour. We encourage respect for other people and urge our readers to take an active part in the community."

Take A Break readers are interested in relationships and raising children, diet and fitness and making the most of their money. It's an old-fashioned, gritty but highly successful menu.

Even if *Take A Break* isn't to your taste, it illustrates that ordinary women and their problems are eminently readable – and sellable.

Top topics for parents

Daphne Razazzan, former editorial director at Dorling Kindersley, says that parenting is a hot topic for writers. There's no degree you can do in it, no one knows anything about it until it happens to them. We get almost all of our information from other parents, frequently passed on through women's magazines, which are an important source of responsible advice on parenting. They always have been.

"Write about parenting in a direct and accessible way, and a friendly way," Daphne says. "Parenting is a blank sheet, an adventure – no new parent really knows what to do. Because of the nuclear family, parents don't have a lot of close support from relatives. They need information and reassurance badly."

Maybe one of these parenting ideas will be right for you to try this weekend – but decide first which magazine you want to send it to. Make sure your style fits theirs.

▶ Parenting on a small budget

▶ Teaching children good manners

▶ Rural parents

▶ Parents whose grown-up children come back to live with them

▶ Older parents

▶ Parents of adopted toddlers or young children

▶ New parents learning how to handle babies

▶ Parents struggling with disability or illness

▶ Parents working from home

▶ Hints on disciplining children

Picture this!

Smiling pictures of you and your child will improve your chances of getting published in a women's magazine. For the photo, dress your child in pristine but inexpensive, one-colour clothes – brand new socks, plain T-shirt or a new baby outfit. Buy them in Tesco or Primark. Nothing will spoil the picture more than a glimpse of a dingy nappie, white socks that have gone grey or a T-shirt with an inappropriate and all-too-readable message. Your picture doesn't have to be taken with a digital camera: clear prints are fine.

Winning ideas

I defy you not to get a feature for a women's magazine from at least one of my ideas this weekend! Try these:

▶ List five things in your day that please you – and five that annoy.

▶ How do you and your partner differ in the kitchen?

▶ Would going on holiday alone frighten you? Or do you prefer it?

▶ Supermarket shopping – do you secretly love it?

▶ What do you do to free yourself from the 'afternoon slump'?

- ▶ How much of the day do you spend thinking about food?
- ✂ ▶ What's your first thought when you wake up? ✂
- ▶ If you could have only one breakfast dish for the rest of your life, what would it be?
- ▶ Ever spent time tracking down old boy/girl friends on Friends Re-united?
- ▶ How tidy is your home – honestly?
- ▶ Would you secretly like to live alone, seeing your much-loved partner maybe three times a week or so?
- ✂ ▶ What one simple luxury would change your life?
- ▶ If you could live your life again, would you have children the second time around?
- ▶ Was school mainly a waste of time, except for learning to read, write and add up?

Still looking for an idea? This relaxation exercise might help:

Sit quietly and focus on just thinking, feeling for an idea. Let thoughts flow in and out of your brain – let them come and go. Rising to the surface, gradually, will be the one idea you want to write about.

When it's taken shape, get it down on paper and make a few notes around it – develop the idea a little, no matter how simple it is.

> ### *Think DOSH:*
>
> Direct
> Ordinary
> Simple and
> Honest

Think small

Some writers strive for effect by using long words and needlessly complicated sentences crammed with many ideas and sub-clauses. Wrong. Or they feel they need an exceptional story, an amazing experience to write about. Yes, that sometimes helps, but usually it's day-to-day worries and topics that get readers hooked. I don't think domestic detail is trivial anyway – from these minutes and hours comes our whole life. What do we enjoy and what drives us mad?

It's the small and simple things that count. That's where you'll create – and sell –your articles for women's magazines.

Go to market

▶ Don't forget – marketing is vital.

▶ Include some non-returnable cuttings, but not too many; no more than five or six will do.

▶ Attach a brief CV showing your interests.

▶ Do not forget to provide your e-mail address and phone number, as well as your postal address.

▶ If you are a subscriber or are on the magazine's Reader Panel, say so.

▶ Include a small, non-returnable picture of you, perhaps with your child or family.

Got your preferred women's magazines in front of you? Think of an idea, do some notes, write and finish an article this weekend.

9 – Write for your local glossy

'The local glossy magazine tells you a great deal about the people who live in the area – how they spend their working time, and their free time. Writers have only to keep their eyes and ears open to have articles accepted for local magazines.'

~David Kernek, magazine and newspaper editor.

I bet that at your home right now there are one or two local magazines lying round. They could well be the glossy, upmarket city or county magazines that get pushed through the letterboxes in areas where the publishers know there are sufficient upmarket homes. This weekend, you can put together a short piece for one of them, along with a list of ideas for future features.

Having a feature published in a local magazine was my first step into the magazine world. I will never cease to be grateful to the *North East Times*, in Newcastle upon Tyne, for sending me a letter that began, "We are pleased to inform you", went on to ask for a monthly article, and offered a fee of £30 for every one of them! I'd sent them three ideas and some examples of my work, suggesting I could do a monthly feature for them – never thinking they'd say yes. But not only did I get the £30 every month, they also gave me a photo by-line!

Every month I came up with a topic, which was relevant to the city – anything from a profile of The Queen, who was making a visit to Newcastle, to a feature about a stately home in the area. I saw that feature as a 'market stall' to show off my work. The payment was low, but I didn't hesitate when the magazine offered me a regular slot; it was the best opportunity. My feature spot in *North East Times* lasted 12 years.

Later I became editor of a regional 'homes' magazine in South West England, and that also taught me a lot. Features about people and their homes need to have a point, so I would select for interview men and women – and it was mostly women – with something to say that wasn't just about the colour of their curtains. I did spreads on an author in a seaside flat who would talk about how she'd arranged her writing room, a chef who talked about his kitchen, designed by him, and a musician talking about his detached home in a forest.

It's tempting to underestimate the power of the local magazine – they're primarily advertising platforms, and they're given away. But they can be a gateway to much greater things. Being published in them gives you great cuttings. They do well on design, so that will make your work eye-catching when you send cuttings to editors.

Making the pitch

Selling work to your local city or county magazine could be easier than you think. As a writer, you have a great advantage: you live in the area and know it well. The publishers and editors will snap up good work from local writers. The fee they offer could be low – they won't fund Caribbean holidays – but many readers will see you in it, and some of them will contact you with suggestions for other features. If you supply good photographs as well, that makes you even more useful from the editor's point of view.

City magazines are very different from their county cousins, although some elements are the same. In city magazines, the main elements are property and homes, entertainment and the arts, plus food, wine and fashion. County magazines are more staid, but they're still interesting – farming, rural events, wildlife, environmental issues, country politics and organic food.

First, read the magazine carefully. You'll be able to tell the age of the readership they're aiming at. Is it about clubbing and fashion, or historic sites and smart restaurants? Are the features about local aristocrats and retired judges, or restaurant owners and fashion designers? Are the reviews of rock music or classical CDs? Thought-provoking fiction or local history books? Are the food columns for people who'll think nothing of spending £70 a head, or do they review Greasy Spoon cafés best known for their all-day breakfasts? The key to making a successful pitch is understanding what the magazine wants.

Send a brief covering letter with the piece you do this weekend, plus a few lines about yourself, and a small, head-and-shoulders picture which in the trade is known as a mugshot. And if you can come up with them, set out three brief outlines for extra ideas. Include any cuttings of articles – no more than four – you have previously had published. Even if you have no cuttings, that won't be a handicap if they like your idea and your approach. The editor will be looking for originality; an understanding of the magazine; a knowledge of the city; accuracy and reliability.

My local glossies… and yours

In Bath, where I live, there are two first-class glossies. Both are distributed free, and their content could, with a little adaptation here and there, be replicated in magazines for any similar historic city in Britain.

This was what *Bath Magazine* had in its September 2005 issue: Notes on a city district that is moving upmarket – and where property values are rising; arts and exhibitions listings; a Jane Austen festival; life and times of an 18th century Bath artist; days out for families; education – a guide to private schools; eating out; health and beauty; a detailed walk through the city; pets corner; and a 'My Bath' column.

This was the package provided by its rival, *Bath Life*: A brief summary of significant news events, for readers who no longer buy the local evening paper; 30 pages of property advertisements; a profile of a nearby Cotswold village: bygone Bath; a money page; a car review; a look at one historic street; wine and food; health and beauty; furnishings; and an informative guide to finding out about the history of your house.

Oh yes… and both magazines had shopping sections!

The simplest idea could make you a feature in your local magazine.

In the *Bath Magazine* of July 2006, there was an excellent article by Andrew Swift on Rail Rover train tickets, which offer unlimited rail travel in the South West of England. These tickets are so under-promoted by train companies that even their own staff sometimes deny they exist – because they don't know about them.

All Andrew had done was keep his eyes and ears open – he must have seen an ad for them somewhere, or heard someone mention them – research the website, add his own colour and detail, find out actual train times and package it all in an easy-to-read, factual but entertaining article. This is exactly the kind of article you could write from your desk in an afternoon.

This is how he begins his feature:

> *Rail Rover tickets, offering unlimited rail travel in designated areas, are one of the greatest travel bargains around.*
>
> *You're unlikely to see them advertised at stations. Ticket office and inquiry staff often look puzzled when asked about them. Rail Rovers have been around for years, but today's operating companies tend to keep quiet about them, preferring to push more expensive ticket options. But, armed with the information in this article, stand your ground. If you enjoy travelling by train, and have an eye for a bargain, you'll be glad you did.*

Simply by researching the train routes and time-tables, he advises:

> *You can even change at St Austell for a bus to the Eden project, leaving Bath at 9.01 and getting back at 21.51, you can spend five hours looking round the site. End of the line is Penzance with its station on the waterfront, looking across to St Michael's Mount. Catching the trains suggested above, it is possible to have over five hours in Penzance, with the added bonus of a return trip over on one of the world's great railway lines.*

He concludes:

> *There is no guarantee Rail Rovers will be available for ever… now is a good time to explore what is left of the rail network. For some days out with a difference, take advantage of one of the greatest – and least known – travel bargains around, get out the maps, pick up some timetables and prepare to rove the rails.*

Andrew's feature is perfectly targeted at the city magazine… and at city readers. It:

▶ offers a new idea for spending free time, even one day

▶ offers a useful money-saving tip – city dwellers are always short of cash

▶ winkles out a special deal that rail companies like to 'forget'

▶ does all the legwork for the reader

▶ gears the subject to the city – trains leave from and return to Bath

▶ gives the websites for Rail Rovers, train timetables, even the Eden Project in an add-on box

▶ is topical – urging readers to take advantage now, before these tickets vanish

Local travel, transport and any deals – well-known or well-concealed – for residents are always worth exploring or re-visiting. Remember that new people are always moving into your neighbourhood, so topics will be new to them.

Top tip

City people are always looking for ideas! Write about new things to do. If you can combine these ideas with a money-saving angle, you're on to a winner.

You could adapt all and any of these topics to fit the city you live in. Good angles to mine would be:

- A detailed, nostalgic look at a part of the city, illustrated with then and now pictures. The 'thens' might come from your own family. If they've lived in the city a long time, they'll have pictures.

- The life and times of any city hero – musician, writer, actor, architect.

- Health and beauty – a look at a local spa, leisure centre or therapy centre, with contact details and prices.

- Street markets, and their history.

- Interesting property that's for sale – with a summary of its history. I found a dilapidated town house in Bristol that had been owned by the local theatre manager. Many actors had stayed there. All I did was look in the window of an estate agent and note that the house was next to the theatre stage door.

- Antiques, gardening, pets – you do need to have some insider knowledge, but you also have to write in a friendly, accessible way. You'll have tips and advice to pass on.

- Food and wine – you'll need to have some credentials, but that could mean being a Women's Institute cake champion or a school dinner lady. It could even mean being a man who hates cooking, but has two standby dishes he can manage and a list of his favourite city takeaways. Magazines are looking for 'real' local writers, not food snobs.

- Family and kids columns – just being a parent who can write would suffice. There's no training you can do in it; we're all experts or trying to be. Most people with young or teenage children crave advice – if only to read it and then reject it.

Here's some more practical topics for the city reader. You can write about these if you have experience of them, or can research them.

- Roof gardens – have you or a friend got one? Tips on roof gardening?

- Housework tips for dual-career couples.

- Patio decoration and maintenance – easy suggestions.

- Job training in the city.

- Leisure courses.

- City walks and churches.

- Dinner parties in a hurry.

- Wine evenings on a budget.

- Raising funds for charity.

- Four weekends – four parts of the city to explore in a month.

- Writing courses at the local college – could you do one and write about it?

> ▶ Budget entertainment – which cinemas have cheap tickets on Mondays? Which restaurants offer cut-price meals, and where's the city catering college with its nearly-free cordon bleu menus? Where can you buy the city's cheapest cappuccino? Where are the training schools for hairdressers and beauticians, with their budget prices?

There's always the possibility of finding a local angle on a national topic.

You could find a local angle on:

▶ City crime and the low numbers of policemen on the beat

▶ Popularity of wine buying, wine as a hobby and the increase of wine merchants tasting rooms in cities

▶ What's done for the homeless in your city, in summer and in winter

▶ Salsa and rock n roll classes – their new popularity among older people

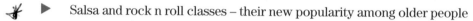

Property matters...

Property is a huge pull. You could write about:

▶ City houses with a history – sometimes they're houses that once were chapels or small schools

▶ Former warehouses that are loft apartments

▶ Houses that are eco-friendly – with solar heating and re-cycled water

▶ Georgian villas with Romanesque swimming pools hidden in the basements

But don't forget that you'll will need pictures to send in with your feature. Find details from property agents: start by looking in their windows and through the property sections of local papers. There's probably a property guide or two offered free to residents. If estate agents know you are writing about one of their properties, they will help with pictures and details – it's free advertising for them.

...and people do, too

Think about doing profiles of people with unusual jobs – in crafts, arts or property maintenance. Or interview a bus driver, postman, librarian or street cleaner – what's their job like? What's their unique view of the city?

I'd like to see a diary written by a single person moving into their first home; or a retired couple living the work-free life for the first time; or a piece about living well in the city on a budget with all the discounts and residents' tickets you can get. You could do any of these from your desk.

> ### Top tip
>
> It's pointless to write about events and places outside the city, unless you can see a section that's geared to trips out. And remember: city writing is all about doing, not just reading – city people are always involved in change and business. They always need cash-saving deals. Be practical. City people want ideas.

Style matters… and size!

What sort of style should you aim for? The better your English, the better your piece. Most city magazines go for a neutral rather than cosy style: you might well look at *The Times* for a guide.

Length? I would say 700 to 750 words for a one-page piece, no more than 1,200 for a two-page spread.

Read the ads

Advertisements – large and small – tell you quite a bit about readership. In the Bath magazines, the emphasis is on services to help busy families (cleaning, laundry, childcare) and on luxuries to beautify homes (wood flooring, roll top baths, slate floors for kitchens). And there's health and beauty services, some of them extremely expensive. There are personal fitness instructors and Thai beauty treatments. Not interested? What about Pilates, tooth whitening and personal chefs – they all go to show that the magazines want to reach readers who are cash rich and time poor.

But my own theory is that in this city, Bath, there are sophisticated people who live in high-value houses but don't necessarily have much disposable income. They're after quality on a budget. And this is true of most people in most cities. City living is expensive – city dwellers relish ways to hang on to their cash.

Yet the relationship between well-off and poor is intertwined in the city, not compartmentalised as it might be in the suburbs. So I have thought about trying to interview one or two of the many homeless people who beg in the most fashionable streets of Bath, making me feel guilty as I hurry by every day. What would it be like to be one of them? I can't be the only one who worries about both giving, and not giving. Written from the right angle, this might appeal to a city magazine. You could also interview arts and fashion students living on a budget – how do they get their 'look' on limited cash?

How do first time home buyers manage to fund mortgages for city centre properties sold at sky-high prices? City centre buskers – the good ones – are another topic that would interest editors. Artists showing their first exhibitions – what do they choose and what's their work all about?

But all these are ideas for later on; for this weekend, tackle something you can do without leaving your home.

Local places

Think local places, but not the cliché places – think of alternatives: secret corners, something different, a new twist on an old venue. This is what will attract the attention of the busy editor.

Do more than the guidebooks! One of the worst things you can do is re-write the guidebook. You must do a little extra research. Make a personal visit, talk to people there. If you are writing about a stately home, go there and talk to the people who own or manage it; they'll often have extra material for you. They'll be pleased that someone is interested enough to take the trouble to visit them, instead of just regurgitating a guidebook.

My rule of three

Never inundate editors with very long lists of ideas, and resist the temptation to fire off a new batch just after few have been turned down. Always do ideas in sets of threes – a one-line summing up plus a paragraph explaining what your feature will do. Let the editor know how the feature would be illustrated. Do you have good pictures? If not, can you take them? If not, do you know who can supply them?

Here's an example of ideas I might pitch to a local magazine when I send in an article:

Backstage at the Roman Baths

A look at the below-stairs staff – the guides, ticket sellers, cleaners and antiquities experts who keep one of the world's most fascinating and historic sites afloat. The city centre complex is open to the public every day, except one, in the year – but how?

Alternative Bristol

The smart boutiques of Clifton and the shopping malls of Broadmead are well known – but what about the ancient herb market and the Eskimo Church? There are intriguing places to visit within a few minutes of the city centre…

The Easter fair

There's a lot of history attached to Easter fairs. A look at the past – and the present – of the traditional fair with its dodgem cars and candyfloss. What do the Ghost Train mechanics and the tombola children do in the winter?

Painting with words

Here are some ways you can go deeper in your writing this weekend and make your articles for local magazines more instantly appealing: spend an hour on this. You'll need some of the weekend newspapers.

Look at the political cartoons in newspapers and magazines. Yes, they're drawing, and you're writing, but you can learn a trick or two from cartoonists, who translate complex issues into simple, instantly understandable, ideas. See how they create a cast of characters identified and embellished with fine yet telling details – you can use this technique in your writing. It's often the small things that delineate people – maybe a button-hole flower, the style of clothes they choose, their physical stance. Notice what the cartoonists notice, then use that sort of detail in your feature. For example, when you meet someone, add one or two of these small details to describe him or her, instead of falling back on conventional and over-used adjectives such as 'friendly' or 'distinguished'.

If you are doing a profile piece about a business person, take a look at:

▶ The items they have on their desk – could be toys, writing tools, piles of books, papers and files, family photographs – or nothing at all.

▶ Does he or she smoke? What kind of cigarettes are they? Is the lighter a Mickey Mouse one, maybe a gift from a child? Or is it in the provocative shape of a woman in a bikini? All this is good detail. Use it.

▶ Hair style – the academic with a grey ponytail, the young woman writer with a dramatic short crop, the glamorous middle-aged woman with bright red hennaed bob. The way people wear their hair says something about them – it's a statement.

Never forget – no choice, however small, is entirely accidental. And readers love detail.

Get the close-up shot

Take a magnifying glass to your subject. Zoom in on one aspect of it. If you are writing a piece about a stately home, instead of conventionally reporting the number of visitors it attracts, or the cups of tea sold in the café, find out how many servants have lived there. What were their lives like? By picking out an unusual or different aspect and going deeper into it, you add irresistible details to your features and your chances of selling them will be so much greater.

Add these to your writing if you are doing a piece on a stately home.

▶   A paragraph about the staff party – what they have to eat, typical gifts from the owners, who attends from 'the family', what games are played?

▶   Who looks after the flowers in the house? How many vases are there to be filled?

▶   What are the challenges in keeping such a big house heated – and clean?

The balancing act...

Readers want some light relief, even in highly factual pieces. In magazine features, you can get balance by dividing up the information you want to convey and allocating, say, four or five paragraphs for each. Then look at them and make sure there's contrast – some paragraphs are light, some serious; some are numbers-based, some are about ideas.

Here's an example of how to achieve balance, with serious and light detail:

Topic – Stately home
Intro – Number of loo rolls and flower vases, brief description of the house:

> *"At Cherry View House, which is 500 years old this year, there are 74 flower vases in its 43 rooms, and they're crammed in spring with roses and bluebells from its lush, 8,000-acre Cornish estate. Every day, the vases – many of them antiques – are topped up and the blooms refreshed. More prosaically, the house, built as a Royal country residence and now a showpiece Elizabethan house that's open to the public, gets through more than 6,000 white loo rolls a year... a refinement unheard of when its foundation stones were laid."*

The structure of the rest of the feature might look something like this:

▶   A brief, outline history of the house

▶   A few facts about the family

- ▶ Highlights for visitors

- ▶ Staff angles

- ▶ End with some quirky, tragic or humorous facts from the house's history, and a sentence or two on its probable future. Are any major developments planned? Are there any planning issues that could affect the house?

Colour up

One of the main problems young writers have is that they don't use the sufficiently wide range of adjectives available in the English language. They tend to fall back on the same, much overworked ones. For some reason I don't quite understand, new writers are nervous of them. But adjectives are there to be used – don't be scared of them. They add colour, vitality, polish and gloss to your phrasing.

You can describe the people you meet, describe their appearance and their personality – robust, elegant, formal, relaxed, cheerful, shy – these are all non-contentious adjectives that can be used for different situations. Describe places as not just beautiful or grand. They could be graceful, oppressive, sombre, strange, theatrical, discordant, well-ordered – there are so many adjectives you could use. Find ones that are not used so often, but are instantly understood.

Make a habit of always adding two or three new adjectives to any magazine article that you write.

Now you've learned what to write for your local glossy magazines. You know what they need. Ideas are coming to you even now! By Sunday evening you could have your feature, and a short list of extra ideas, ready to send to editors.

Top tip

Boxes and sidebars – like this one! – will help your piece. List:

- ▶ Tips
- ▶ Do's and don'ts
- ▶ Five things to look out for
- ▶ Four things not to miss

If your feature is about a distinguished local pensioner, ask him or her to give their five tips for a happy life, and list them in a sidebar.

Give your feature one or two extra layers – think of a couple of bolt-ons. For example, if you are covering a city district, suggest four other places of interest nearby. Suggest three budget places to eat, or six events that take place there. With a gardening piece, add a box about an ideal low-maintenance plant, then add three alternatives. If you're writing about giving a kid's party, outline your standby children's tea menu, then add four other choices. Give readers plenty of ideas for everything.

10 – And the rest... hobbies, work and food

'Magazines aim to balance familiarity and surprise'

~ Nick Gibbs, Future Publishing

As a magazine writer, you can make any field your own – just by having a passion for it. Let that passion show; let that commitment shine through and you can write articles based on your own enthusiasms. You do not have to have a degree in the topic. In fact, it's usually better if you don't! There aren't very many academics who can write well enough for magazines.

When there's something you are passionate about, you read all you can about it, research it, and experience it. But there are some fields you already know inside out, back to front and upside down – your work, family and hobbies. You, and only you, are the expert here. You have an unlimited reservoir of personal experience to mine and from which to create magazine articles. And over the next 48 hours you're going to!

There's plenty of choice as to what you write about. I have selected some of the main magazine arenas, which always require features – work, hobbies and interests, and food. So this weekend I would like you to try one of these:

▶   A feature based on your hobby or interest – it could be antiques, sewing, music, stamp-collecting, gardening, even writing – anything

or

▶   An article based on your work, or work that you know about – it could be something a family member does, or did

or

▶   A foodie article – it could be about anything from putting together a week's vegetarian lunchboxes for kids, planning a supper for friends for £30, feeding a foreign student, making award-winning chutney or doing a day course in easy cooking for men. You don't have to be Jamie Oliver!

Get a hobby – and write about it

The format for special interest articles for magazines doesn't vary greatly. You talk about your subject and what it's meant to you. You give useful tips for readers. You offer them benefits from reading your article. You can tell them about mistakes you've made – so they can avoid them. You might have a few facts and figures – maybe from new research, an official report, a news story, which you can mention or even use it as the 'peg' on which to hang your feature. Here's an example:

In an *Eve* magazine feature headlined *Eat Your Own Garden*, Dominic Utton writes:

> *What do you think of when you read the words "growing your own vegetables"? Ruddy-cheeked Ma Larkins at a country fair? Old men in ancient sweaters digging in higgledy-piggledy allotments by the train tracks? Tom and Barbara Good? Think again.*

He continues:

> *Growing your own is just as likely to be done by professional thirty-somethings with children and limited free time... allotments are enjoying a level of popularity not seen since the Second World War (when we were urged to 'dig for victory'). According to the Allotments Regeneration Initiative, women are the fastest growing group of allotment holders, renting around 60,000 plots in the UK.*

> *My wife, Heidi, and I took on an allotment last year armed with an old Alan Titchmarsh book and a load of enthusiasm. The sense of pride we felt in our first batch of runner beans was akin to that of new parents... on our site there's a real sense of community. The committee holds a harvest festival with curry made from allotment veg and a barrel of beer courtesy of the local brewery. It's a chance to get pleasantly drunk and talk about composting in the sunshine... and how often do you get to do that?*

After briefly commenting on the huge amount of greenhouse gases that are released into the atmosphere as vegetables are transported across the globe to our local supermarkets, Dominic sums up proudly:

> *By way of contrast, the peas Heidi and I are growing release precisely zero pollutants on their journey from our allotment to our saucepan.*

And he concludes:

> *It's good for you, saves you money, provides a sense of achievement and saves the planet. Why on earth would you not want to grow your own?*

He's followed the classic outline for a hobbies feature:

▶ An introduction that instantly draws readers in – they don't have to be gardening fans. It has a sentence that shows the old stereotype of gardeners has changed – to include readers of *Eve*.

▶ Statistics that lend a point to his feature – the figures from the Allotment Regeneration Initiative demonstrating that women are now the main allotment holders.

▶ Personal details… his wife Heidi… their limited knowledge of gardening, "an old Alan Titchmarch book", combined with their enthusiasm… the thrill they felt with their runner beans, like parents of newborns.

▶ Useful tips for readers – why not have an allotment party?

▶ A reference to current affairs – greenhouse gases, and the way he and Heidi, thanks to their allotment, are not contributing to them.

▶ An interesting challenge to readers, with the benefits made clear – help the planet and grow your own!

None of this is new: I was writing magazine articles on the benefits of allotments 30 years ago. But the way he writes it is fresh, personal and engaging. He's writing as an allotment holder, and not as an expert gardener.

Words which sell

If you're writing a hobbies article, these are useful words and phrases to include:

Think again	*Wrong!*
These days…	*Make money with*
You're an expert too	*No qualifications needed*
Why not?	*Imagine…*
Reap some rewards	*Gain new skills*
Sense of achievement	*Benefits*
Be happy	*Stress-free*
Make new friends	*Easier than you think*
Never be bored	*No age limit*
Fill your weekend	*Addictive*
Absorbing	*Refreshing*
Unlimited pleasure	*In your own time*
Try a taster	*Go on a leisure course*
Good for you	*Good for the planet*

Find your niche

The other kind of hobby writing involves turning your interest into a niche market. As I've said already, some of my best articles on Greece come not from archaeologists or professors of Greek literature but from gifted enthusiasts.

Rob Adams writes about music for *Greece* magazine, but he's a special needs advisor, not an academic:

> *Do you ever wonder how much of what we value in life we come across by accident? Lovers, jobs, interests – there are so many aspects of our lives seemingly governed by chance. It was the sheer chance of being given a Greek compilation CD that led me to the voice of Eleni Tsaligoloulou. It has a totally bewitching – and very addictive – quality. Born in Naousa in Northern Greece, she started singing at an early age, often accompanied by her brother. She is classically trained, having studied at the Greek Conservatory in Thessaloniki. She made her first professional singing appearance in 1985, while still attending the conservatory.*

Here's another example of Rob's fresh and easy style:

> *When I decided to buy some Greek music in Greece for the first time, I found myself in conversation with a couple of Greeks in their early 20s. I asked if they could recommend some Greek music. Their open-eyed response was identical to the one I've found myself inadvertently adopting over the years when asked the same question: what sort? It's the same if you were asked about English music. What sort? Vaughan Williams? Dusty Springfield? The Clash? The field is so wide.*

> *They took me to their friend's record shop and a few hours later, I emerged with a CD of Vasilis Papakonastadinou's greatest hits. It is not traditional (a much misused word). It is electric/acoustic rock music. And it's great.*

He's writing as an ordinary Joe who just happened to love Greek music, has bought CDs, took advice and gradually built up a wide and deep knowledge. But – he's still not a musicologist! He's not a music professor! He's a guy with a flair for writing about his hobby. You can do it too.

Work out!

Work is a marvellous topic to mine for magazine articles. Most people work at something, so you already have a captive audience.

What's one of the first things you often want to ask about someone new? Could it be what work they do, what jobs they've had? Knowing what people do – and how they do it, put up with it, or feel about it – is an endless source of interest and fascination. Writing about work is one of the new and expanding areas in magazine writing. And what do most people tell you about their job? Often, how stressful it is. Work-connected stress has spawned a whole new area for the magazine writer.

Writing about people and their jobs has become an expanding market – I call it 'workplace writing'. Curiosity and fascination with the world of work – its pleasures, pitfalls, possibilities, miseries and delights – provides a major plank in all our lives.

You could write about your job this weekend.

It doesn't have to be personal – you can find an angle, create a 'case history' using a real person with a made-up name. Here's an example I wrote for *Woman Alive* magazine:

> *When stress at work causes you to sit and seethe, or keeps you awake at night fuming, how easy is it to hang on to those Christian principles? Martha Holland, a 43-year-old secretary in Victoria, began to dread going to a job she'd previously enjoyed. She realised it was because a new colleague upset her. He brought in a cassette player and played pop music as he worked.*
>
> *"I just could not concentrate – I found the whining noise, though quiet, infuriating," she says.*
>
> *"I mentioned it and he said he would turn it off when I asked. But I was having to ask nearly every day. I just wanted to smack him. I became quite stressed about it, even though I like music. I just didn't want it on while I tried to work."*

I used a friend – and her difficult situation – for this case study, but I changed her name. You'll have plenty of friends whose problems – and triumphs – you could use for work-related articles. Or you could use true stories from your own life.

For *Woman Alive* magazine, this was the style that would fit. I went on to talk about work in general and how much stress it can cause these days… plus some practical tips – based on my own experience in the workplace – for handling it.

Honest work

There is no job you can't write about. You might be a sales assistant, a call centre operator, a cashier in a supermarket, a receptionist, a B&B landlady, an actress, a poet, a secretary, a waitress, a cleaner or a cook. The list is almost without end.

Don't forget the basic structure. Cull a few relevant statistics from newspapers if the feature needs them. Find an angle – it can be as simple as the price of office sandwiches, workplace noise levels, the pressure people are under, the lack of time to do things properly, the continual goal-setting, uncomfortable and crowded offices, inadequate pension provision – you'll find something.

Be honest, frank – but not angry. Add your personal tips for readers on dealing with the problems you're writing about. Mention any useful websites.

Of course, you can always write about someone else's job. Someone in your family perhaps – your mother, brother or uncle?

Jan Elford wrote in *The Lady* about her grandfather's job – as a milkman who first delivered the milk by jugs, with a horse and cart.

She started her feature – headlined *Bottled Memories* – with a nugget of topical information:

> *It was recently reported that the British pinta was under threat from the EU Parliament, which was considering replacing bottled foodstuffs with cartons. In 1921, my grandfather Frederick John Taylor started a dairy business in South London…by horse and cart he travelled round calling out "Mi-iulk!" Out they would come with jugs, bowls and money and he ladled milk into their containers. Finding this rather tedious he investigated the idea of delivering milk in bottles. He became one of the first dairymen to buy his own distinctive wide-necked bottles – he was an entrepreneur of his time.*

After the war, her father took over the business:

> *Always up at 3 a.m. when the milk churns were delivered, he would start out about 5 a.m on his round. After breakfast he would repeat the procedure with more churns of the drum. A lasting childhood memory was seeing the milk form a foamy froth as it reached the top of the drum, resembling a milkshake. Often I was treated to a glass of this beautiful frothy milk skimmed off the top.*

> *How I regret not keeping a Taylor milk bottle and white tab top as a keepsake, for they were such an important part of my early days in the dairy.*

Remember – cull statistics or facts from newspapers if the feature needs them. Find an angle, no matter how simple. Make it personal. Give detail. Add tips for readers – here she's offering the idea of readers hanging on to family work memorabilia, because they're things that can disappear from society. They can become museum pieces – you'd wish you'd kept these small mementoes of a bygone age.

Have you a friend, or is there someone living in your town or city, who has succeeded in their work despite a handicap? Mention the disability in a matter of fact way, and focus on their success.

The following is the introduction to a feature I wrote for *Woman Alive* on blind entrepreneur Liz Jackson, who runs Great Guns Marketing. I also sold the piece to *The Guardian*'s Office Hours section. For *Woman Alive*, there was more on Liz; for *The Guardian*, extra detail on a Government scheme providing free personal assistants to disabled people working in offices.

> *Seven years ago Liz Jackson, 31, launched her telemarketing company Great Guns with a £100 grant and £4,000 loan from the Prince's Trust. Today Liz, who is totally blind, employs 100 people. The company turnover is around £1.5m and there are eight regional branches and franchises.*
>
> *… as for being blind "I ignore it. It's a practical issue only," says Liz. "In a telemarketing career, the main tools are voice and ears. When I meet a new client, I introduce myself and just say 'By the way I'm blind – that's why I'll be hanging onto my PA Pete's arm'. "*

In any feature that centres on the success someone has made of their work – overcoming a personal challenge – focus on their approach to their work, and not on the disability itself. Quiz them for tips on how they approach the job. They will give you tips that will be of use to anyone who does a similar job and wants to do well at it – and that's what will make your feature valuable.

Women's magazines are increasingly writing about people who have set up their own businesses, maybe after having worked as employees in the corporate world for some time. But jobs don't have to be posh or professional or high profile to make them marketable for the freelance magazine writer. If you have set up your own small business, you have the ideal opportunity for writing about it. Readers will want the bad as well as the good, so include a panel of five things you'd wished you'd done, and five things you're pleased you've done, business-wise, of course!

If you want some ideas on writing about your own business, take a look at *The White Ladder Diaries* by Ros Jay (The White Ladder Press £9.99 www.whiteladderpress.com). Ros and her husband Richard were both writers – books and magazine articles – when they decided to set up their own publishing company from home. The book charts their progress from brainwave to books, with a wealth of invaluable tips. Written in an engaging diary form, it's a good example of the honesty and vitality you can inject into just writing about yourself and your own business. Ros talks candidly about the mistakes they made as well as the triumphs – and about her own emotions when things went badly. It's a business how-to with the must-read-on of a novel. See if this is a style you can adapt for an article about your own business or job.

Food, food, food

Can you write about food? Most surely, yes. And as you should have picked up from me by now – you don't have to be an expert! You don't need a Cordon Bleue diploma! You don't need to have gone to catering college!

There are so many opportunities for getting into the specialist food and wine magazines and the general interest women's titles.

Crafty cookery tips

When writing about any aspect of cooking:

▶ Use colloquial, breezy language, not serious catering-ese. You can 'whizz' things in a blender, 'plonk' things in the oven, 'blast' them with cream or sugar – write the way you speak.

▶ Don't edit out your cooking mistakes – readers love to hear about them, and how you cooked your way out of them.

▶ Readers travel more, so it's OK to use exotic ingredients and ideas. Make sure they can purchase them here, give website and mail order addresses, telephone numbers etc. Give readers information they can use.

▶ Yes, you can quote from other writers' cookbooks – a small extract of a few sentences is fair usage – but you should attribute the quote with book's title, author and publisher.

▶ The more pictures you can offer to go with your feature, the better. Include some of you in an apron, around a dining table with friends and family, in the garden picking herbs – be imaginative and don't be stingy with pictures. Cheap but clear prints are perfectly fine.

▶ If you include recipes, they must be accurate, clear and in the same style throughout – figure and words arrangements mustn't change. Use imperial measures with metric in brackets, or the other way round – according to the magazine's style. But don't keep changing the format.

7 top of the range ideas

1   ARE you a dinner lady or a cook at a supermarket or nursery group, or maybe you've just got small children and have a talent for giving parties for them? Why not write about that?

2   COLLECT old cookbooks from charity shops. Take a theme – war cookery for example, or being thrifty – and how it was done in different times.

3   ROYAL cookery – research the wedding breakfasts organized for The Queen (roast and fine wines), Princess Anne (champagne and crisps for her second wedding, an elaborate spread for her first), Fergie, (a flower-strewn extravaganza) Charles and Camilla (simple but luxurious) and create recipes and tips round them.

4   BUY vintage crockery and cheap old cookery utensils from junk shops; create recipes to fit their age.

5   PICK a sum – £10, £20, or £30 – and plan a dinner party to fit that budget. Yes, it can be done! With lots of tips and hints, this is a winner for a family magazine. Make sure you include a photograph of you and your guests, and the food.

6   WRITE about a memorable meal you had abroad and re-create it at home, giving all of the ingredients and where they can be bought here. The big supermarkets have extensive international food shelves.

7   TRY to live for a week – or even a month! – on the food budget your mother had when she was your age. Remember that food and groceries have actually got cheaper in many ways – shops and supermarkets didn't have BOGOF offers then – and freezers mean we now don't have to cook from fresh every day.

Foodie holiday

Food and wine holidays are increasingly popular – and they're a gift for a writer. You could write about:

▶ A holiday visiting wineries

▶ A wine cruise or tour

▶ A cookery holiday here or abroad

▶ One day spent on a specialist cooking course – seafood recipes or bread making, for example

▶ A day or weekend learning to taste wine

▶ A cocktails workshop or a coffee-making seminar

▶ A special skill you learn on a weekend course – could be baking bread, icing cakes, Christmas cookery, puddings, children's cookery

▶ Learning your way a round a cheese board in France

Toolbox tips

INVEST in a basic reference book or two.

SEE what's already on the shelves in Waterstone's or Borders. Is there an 'idiot's guide' or a basic primer, or simple coursebook, on your subject? Don't resent the £9.99 or whatever it is – this is a worthwhile investment.

KEEP buying books on your subject including old ones from charity shops. Contrasting old techniques with new could make you a feature.

CHECK the magazines and yearbooks published on your subject. It may be worth a subscription to one – and this in itself may carry another free book on the topic.

READ newspapers and cut out clippings on your topic.

CHECK the trade press on your subject, go to fairs and workshops on it, pick up leaflets and free magazines.

READ the specialist sections of the national press for news on your topic. Cut out and keep useful stuff.

BUY an address book just for this subject, and begin to build up a contact database.

She did it!

Loretta Proctor (author of *The Long Shadow*, £14.95, www.PublishAmerica. com www.lorettaproctor.co.uk.) recalls the time when her first magazine feature was published – in *The Mountain Astrologer*.

"The joy was indescribable. I danced and sang about the house all day. Completely out of proportion for what it was…I mean you'd have thought I'd won the lottery… but hey, we need a mad moment of celebration in life! My poor friends, who hadn't a clue about astrology, were all obliged to read and marvel over my astonishing literary output and admire my photo, actually in a journal. And I was getting paid in dollars. It all seemed so exotic and grown up. Sadly though, that first moment of pure joy was never experienced again. That's life; we become blasé about everything. But what did I do to get my articles accepted and praised when so many really clever people were writing for these magazines too? (I mean, really learned stuff.) *The Astrological Journal* even ran a poll to find what type of articles its readers enjoyed and to my sincere amazement my piece, *Neptune and the Picture Palaces*', came in as everyone's favourite. Why?

1   Looking back, I see that I always wrote about something I genuinely loved and understood. There has to be a passion about the subject.

2   Many of the articles in the journals I contributed to were too learned and stuffy and often unreadable. Lightness and readability was the key without being flippant or silly, no matter how serious the subject matter.

3   You can become an expert on something and write about that. You will get to know the subject so well, you will easily think of things to say. Research the subject with care. Then put all you have absorbed aside. Really think what your own take is upon the subject in hand, so there will be a new and original voice on the matter.

4   Use short sentences, short paragraphs. One of my first mistakes was lack of brevity. Most people fell asleep before the first paragraph was read. Even I fell asleep.

5   Use beautiful words and elegant sentences that flow smoothly like water. I've been told people may not understand some of the words I like to use. My reply is they should look them up and learn something new. Words are what we writers use just as a painter uses his colours. We need to enchant others occasionally in this dull world.

6   Above all, be determined and have faith in what you have to say. Everyone has a story, message, subject that they love and a yearning to put it before others and inspire them as they have been inspired themselves."

Landmark dates

Editors like special interest features that fit landmark dates, such as an anniversary celebration… but think beyond the conventional dates, such as the anniversary of Nelson's death or J. S. Bach's birth. Look up unusual dates – for example the day Britain metricated its money (it was in 1971), or the year that red phone boxes all but disappeared, or the final day of national service. When did pens and ink wells vanish from schoolrooms? And the typewriter from offices? When did we first start to buy dishwashers? How did we manage before photocopiers; anyone remember carbon paper?

It's the unusual and original angle that will make editors eyes light up.

You, the star

Everyone has a special interest magazine feature that can be extracted from their own life, family history and enthusiasms. And now you know how to tackle them…

11 – Take yourself to market

'A good many young writers make the mistake of enclosing a stamped, self-addressed envelope, big enough for the manuscript to come back in. This is too much of a temptation for the editor.'

~ Ring Lardner

Congratulations! You've done well with your weekend course. I hope you're feeling exhilarated at seeing your efforts building up. Don't worry if you've not completed as much as you wanted to; what you have done is already an achievement, so focus on that, not on what you didn't do. Now is the time to think about taking things forward to more success as a writer. This chapter is about self-belief and marketing yourself – and you can't do one without having the other. Self-belief is crucial if you want to set and achieve writing and marketing goals. It's vital if you want to impress editors.

Your confidence and marketing skills need to be visible. If I have to choose between two articles – both equally well written, both right for the magazine – I will choose the one that is well marketed. The one that doesn't include a stamped, self-addressed envelope! Because, believe me, you will then impress the editor immediately if it's clear that you consider everything you send to be non-returnable.

Magazine editors receive hundreds of submissions and often don't have personal secretaries, or even admin assistants. Plus, these days, you shouldn't really require anything back – it can all be held by you on computer, and you should consider pictures of you as part of your marketing expenses. Marketing is worth doing! It doesn't mean paying a marketing 'expert' to do the work for you. That's a waste of cash. You can do it yourself!

So how do you go about selling yourself? These are musts for your marketing kit:

▶ Business cards – get them free from www.vistaprint.co.uk. You can choose the design and what you want to say on them – and have 150 cards for free; you just pay the postage, about £2.99. Don't ask me how they do it! On your cover letters, give editors your postal and e-mail addresses, your daytime, evening and mobile 'phone numbers – in simple, large type, because contact details in fancy typefaces are hard to read, especially when editors have been reading copy all day. I can't count the number of letters I get from would-be writers with no contact details. The vital one is the phone number – which many would-be writers omit from their letters. This is no way to get published!

▶ A brief biography – ten lines will do.

Mary Jones of Bristol has made six trips to Spanish cities in the last eight years. Her favourite is Seville, where she hopes one day to buy a small apartment. A former primary school teacher, Mary has twins, Leo and Clare, aged 10. She writes on city travel in Spain, with tips on keeping small travellers entertained and interested.

▶ A small selection – no more than five or six – of photostats of cuttings of anything you've had published – readers letters, tips or features.

▶ A stack of passport-size pictures of you that you can send out – and other pictures to go with different types of features. I have photos of me on holiday, with my daughter, at my desk. The picture needs to be geared to what you're writing about. If you are sending a feature to a travel magazine, you might have sunglasses pushed to the top of your head and be wearing a holiday-type T-shirt. Writing a cookery piece? Have yourself photographed wearing an apron and standing by your oven. If you're writing about your work, you could be dressed smartly for business and poised over your laptop. You don't need expensive studio work or the latest in camera technology and ordinary, but clear, prints will do. Ask a family member or friend to take them. It's the way you style your picture and the expression on your face – a smile – that counts.

▶ Christmas cards, which I always send to editors who have used my work during the year. For 60p a pop, it's good PR. And anyway I like these people! I might send a view of Bath, my home city, or I will try to find something with a 'magazine' link, such as a card of an old *Vogue* or *Good Housekeeping* cover. For sending a greeting to a travel editor, I'd send a card bought in a museum shop in Greece, Italy or the USA. I choose cards for my biz contacts carefully, and if I know they don't like or celebrate Christmas – many don't! – I send them a card at New Year instead.

Any writer with a kit like this – all of which can be prepared in advance, in bulk – can market themselves. And their marketing can look professional – and stylish. Why does it matter? It's important because editors see good marketing as a sign that you'll be good to work with. They know they won't have to ask for or explain any extras they might need, such as a brief biography and a photograph to go with the piece you've written. I might like to ask for their help if I hold a phone-in day for readers; if a writer has an understanding of marketing, I know they'll be on my wavelength. I can promote them.

Put simply, the good writer with marketing skills gives me, as an editor, much more value for my magazine.

You're allowed

You can be ready to market if you allow yourself to have the confidence. Where does the allowing come in? Many of my students are reluctant to market themselves, nervous of taking the first step, fearful of what may be involved. Their primary feeling is: "I'm not good enough to market myself. How can I write a short biography about me?" They won't allow themselves to feel strong, brave and confident. They'll tell themselves they'd be showing off, boasting.

Is this you? Do you feel nervous at the thought of marketing yourself? Scared to attempt even a covering letter? Most writers are exactly the same as you. We all have the same fears and anxieties. They're familiar obstacles on the path to success – success many writers feel, perversely, they don't deserve. Why? Perhaps you believe that:

▶ Marketing yourself is the same as showing off

▶ You are a fraud, not good enough, not a 'real' writer

▶ Your friends and family will laugh at you

▶ It's not worth it – the 'why bother?' trap

▶ You're nowhere near as good as other writers

▶ The expense is too much

Here's my answer to all that: rubbish!

▶ Marketing is a conventional, necessary tool for any successful endeavour

▶ You are writing this weekend – you are a writer

▶ They are more likely to be envious

▶ Nothing worth doing is easy

▶ Silence your internal critic

▶ Compare it with the expense of never being published

Think strong

Confidence can slip away when spirits start to fail. When this happens, sit back, let your mind slow down and relax. Take deep breaths. Close your eyes. See yourself marketing a piece, and then looking at a feature you've finished. See the smile on your face as you look at the words on the page. See yourself completing your marketing biography. Make the page and the words on it big, as if on a cinema screen. Enjoy looking at the screen – it's all about you! Feel your own happiness.

Think strong – a tip I was given by Michael, my personal coach, many years ago. I mentioned it in an earlier section of the course. It's held me in good stead. Before I had this tip, I often used to think, when I was writing and marketing, "I'm too tired, I can't go on", or, "No one will use it anyway", or "It's just too hard for me".

Gradually, I began replacing these negative, weak thoughts with, "I'm strong and my body is full of energy", and "My marketing is effective and it will be help to get my articles used", and "People meet incredible challenges – much harder than this!" and "Determination creates stamina. I'm getting a second wind!"

Keep on thinking strong whenever you're tempted to think weak. The more you replace negative thoughts with positive ones, the more easily you'll regain your confidence – all by yourself. What's wonderful about this method is that you don't need anyone to tell you you're strong – you can do it by yourself. And it isn't a quick fix. It lasts. I know confidence coaching works. I've done it for myself.

As I've said, I used to be prone to depression, and along with it came a kind of vanity. If anyone criticised my writing or my way of working, I'd get angry. How dare they? Didn't they know how brilliant I was? How fortunate they were to have me and my incredible genius at their disposal?

Now I've learned to be much more modest – yet at the same time believe more in myself and in my writing. If I encounter criticism or rejection, it doesn't stop me doing more marketing. I try to re-frame my thoughts. Can I use the comments to move my writing forward? Can I re-write or add a new angle to make it suitable? Yes, there's always an initial little flash of anger or annoyance (I haven't yet managed to squash that!) yet nowadays I try not to give in to it. I try to move on, and be positive.

You will get rejection letters occasionally, but you can learn not to let them smash your confidence and stop you marketing

These are my tips for handling one of those thanks-but-no-thanks letters:

1   Don't take it personally – your article may not be suitable for any number of reasons. It could be that the magazine:

▶ Has a feature on the very same topic ready to be published

▶ Has explored this topic in recent issues

▶ Has finished with this topic for a while

▶ Is closing and not taking new ideas

▶ Is changing and not taking this kind of idea now

Or perhaps it's just that the editor has spent his or her freelance feature budget! It happens.

2   If there's a note of advice on your rejection slip, take that as a good sign. The editor is taking time to address you and your work personally – he or she definitely thinks you're worth it. Follow the advice.

It's all about you

Yes, you can write your own biography. And you should attach one to all of your articles. Provided it's short and sweet, what have you got to lose?

It's just eight or ten lines about you, but if you can include a quirky fact or two, that's a draw – it grabs the editor's attention. I sometimes describe myself as a "failed air hostess" or a "Grammar school drop-out" – both true. I encouraged a writing student to include, rather than conceal, the fact he'd spent, in his teenage years, six months as an involuntary guest of Her Majesty. Now he's made a considerable success of both antique dealing and publishing, I didn't think he had to feel guilty any longer for vandalizing a chocolate bar dispensing machine when he was an angry 15-year-old.

Readers and editors love stories of triumph over adversity, achievement after hardship. This is a typical attention-grabbing biography. Don't forget – you write your own short biography, in the third person. It should be confident, attention-grabbing, almost larger than life.

Music shop owner Dermot Smith of Bath spent an entire year out of work ten years ago. "I lived on charity shop buys and music – I listened every day and borrowed CDs from the library. I wrote a job application every week" he recalls. Finally he achieved a sales position in a shop selling jazz and blues music and books. Today he owns his own shop – recently voted the West Country's best blues shop – and also writes on job-hunting. "I left school at 15 and never went to college, but there's not much I don't know about job search," he says.

Words are key

You can also include a short, third person biography of yourself which relates to the feature you are submitting. Don't think of it as boasting. Include key words that will help editors to see how they could place your work. Key words could be mother, specialist, secretary, award winner, magistrate, cook, advanced driver – use words that indicate your knowledge of a specific subject. Three lines will do.

Here's how:

▶ When she researched this feature, mother-of-four Paula Hone loved meeting local gypsies and attending gypsy weddings. She once lived in a caravan and started writing there. She is in her second year of an Open University arts course.

▶ The best part of writing her article, says office temp Jane Jones, was trying out a variety of Far Eastern dishes. She has a certificate in Thai cookery and spent her last holiday backpacking through Indonesia.

▶ John Jenner's best tip for country walkers is to invest in the best and lightest pair of walking boots, not the cheapest. At school, he won awards for athletics and at 56 says he is still "extremely fit". A Post Office counter assistant, he walks at least 40 miles every week.

▶ Looking good and having a varied wardrobe needn't cost the earth, as Kim Cantrell discovered when she explored charity shops in Bath. She managed to buy a new wardrobe for £20 – five pieces. Kim, a Body Shop manager, used to work as a fashion model and is also a prize-winning needlewoman.

Editors welcome such writers – writers with an eye for marketing their work and who can visualize how their work will be displayed in the magazine.

Top tip

The facts you add to your biography should show you are vulnerable, not brilliant (even if you are). But always include awards and achievements, too. Don't go on too long. Eight to ten lines is plenty.

6 mega marketing skills

1   Be businesslike, not wacky or disorganized

2   Set goals

3   Send out non-returnable pictures of yourself

4   Always mention past successes – awards, prizes, distinctions in any field

5   Include clear contact details with everything you send out

6   Take rejection well

---

5 tips for marketing success

1   The more marketing packs you send to magazines, the more you stand to gain. Widen your chances.

2   Don't ask editors to send your cuttings or pictures back – and do not send originals. Always send non-returnable material. These days, many editors do not have secretaries, and they don't welcome extra clerical duties.

3   Include a small picture of yourself so that if you are successful, the editor already has it for a photo by-line. Waiting for pictures to be sent is the bane of any editor's life.

4   If you have a website that showcases examples of your work, don't instruct editors to look at it. I don't think I am alone in feeling faintly annoyed when I ask writers for cuttings and the reply is "go to my website" or "Google my name in". Editors are under colossal pressure, with literally hundreds of details big and small to chase and supervise. So it's much quicker if I can look at cuttings in an instant instead of logging on to a website which, more often than not, takes ages to load or may not even work. Maybe I'll browse it later, but cuttings give me instant information.

5   Every communication – by e-mail, letter, fax or disc should carry your full name, address and phone number, as well as your e-mail address. It's a cardinal rule!

Buy in bulk

It isn't effective to buy small packs of envelopes and postage stamps every so often: bite the bullet and buy them by the hundred if you can. Office stationers will often give discount for bulk buys, and you can buy books of stamps in supermarkets if you don't want to stand in line at post offices. With stationery and stamps at the ready, you're more productive when marketing.

Think in terms of doing larger mail outs – after this weekend, why not send your pack to 20 magazines instead of only five? Go through a writers' yearbook and though *Writers' News* and put Post Its on the pages which have appropriate addresses to which you could market your work. Think big!

Get business cards printed. It's much cheaper to do this now. But make sure your card is clear – no fancy, unreadable typefaces. Choose a large enough typesize for even short-sighted editors to read – and include all of your contact details – e-mail, telephone and address. Attach a card to each mailout. Or have compliments slips printed with the same details, and add these to your pack.

Top tip

Here's one of my best self-marketing tips – have a 'sundown' communications policy. Reply to e-mails and respond to phone calls within 24 hours – then expect to pick up more work. I was amused by a brochure I had from a 'life coach' who boasted that all calls to him – each and every one – would be answered within 24 hours. Except, he said, on Fridays and at weekends!

Killer cover letters

When you send off an article, the cover letter can be as simple as this:

> Susan Smith
> 1, Coburg Villas
> Camden Road
> Bath
> BA1 5JF
> 01225 413331
> susansmith@tiscali.co.uk
>
> Date
>
> Dear Editor (find out his or her name and spell it correctly),
>
> I am enclosing an article on Fountains in Bath which I hope will be of interest to you. If so, of course I'd be able to e-mail it to you.
>
> I'm a special needs teacher, and also I belong to a local writers group. We've had an anthology of articles on local 'alternative' landmarks published, (*Hidden Landmarks of Bath*, £2.99, Anywhere Publishing) with the help of a small grant from Nonesuch Arts Foundation.
>
> My other interests include travel photography and cookery. I was runner-up in the *Travelbag Magazine* national travel writing competition in 2006, with an article on working for a month as a holiday villa cook on the island of Lindisfarne.
>
> A photograph of myself is enclosed – which does not have to be returned. I'd gladly offer more details about myself, and more ideas for features/stories.
>
> I enjoy reading your magazine very much, and I wish you continued success with it.
>
> Kind regards,
>
>
> Susan Smith

Use of words such as happy, gladly and willingly – they suggest a personality that's easy to get on with. Like all of us, editors want to work with cheerful people. It's courteous to include a sincere compliment to the magazine and to wish them success.

This letter refers to an award, a success – vital info for the editor. Some newspaper editors hire only award-winners.

Above all, this letter is short, clear and concise. Experienced editors can often tell just from a covering letter how good the attached feature will be. If your covering letter is clumsy, wordy and dull the chances of the article being a sparkler are remote.

But your covering letter will be perfect!

Food marketing

I liked the application I had from a food writer – she attached to some work examples a well-wrapped home-made biscuit she'd made. When I edited a celebration cake magazine, a would-be writer sent some miniature cakes to me with her cuttings. The value of this kind of marketing is that editors remember you, and your originality and confidence shines through.

Wanting to get into local magazines as a food writer? You could include a few sweets, or a small pot of home-made jam or chutney. Or whatever it is you specialize in. If you are marketing locally, you can deliver by hand.

You need to be a confident cook, not an expert or professional one. You could well be a beginner. Suppose you learned to cook only when you were 40 or 50, or when you retired? That would make a good feature. There are so many angles, so many possibilities in food writing.

Try to exploit it locally. Write to all of the newspapers, local magazines and journals published in your area, using my tips. Maybe you won't be paid a huge fee, but you will achieve profile, be invited to cookery courses and events, sent press releases and samples. Maybe you could even end up with a book of your articles… that often happens to people who write about food, expert or not.

Work at putting together two or three features on different themes, plus four or five ideas. Include some photographs and maybe that tempting morsel – and your chances of success could be surprisingly high.

4 tricks of the trade

Pictures are important – especially good jpegs where the image fills up most of the frame. Take them yourself if you're good at it.

Hints and do's and don'ts always add to your copy.

Advice on buying and selling, especially on e-Bay, goes down a treat.

Shops and markets, with full listings associated with the items you write about, please both readers and advertisers.

How to make friends... and influence editors

▶ Keep a separate database of contacts, with their phone numbers and e-mail addresses. If you keep this on your computer, it will save you time and worry – also you can keep adding to it without digging out your address book. In the specialist writing business, these contacts are vital. When you get help from someone, send them an e-mail or call to say thank you. And, of course, keep all of the contact details of magazines which accept and publish your features.

▶ Send regular updated pictures of yourself – smiling. Each time you write on a subject, offer at least one picture of you with whatever it is you write about – toys, books, teddy bears, babies, wine, your family.

▶ If you are asked to make cuts or add to your story, do it readily, and don't ask for more money!

▶ Proof your work extra carefully, paying attention to the spelling of unusual or exotic names.

▶ Do not assume that the magazine's staff will fill in any spaces for facts or information you haven't been bothered to find. It might be one of the increasing number of magazines produced by one-person staffs!

Skip your way to success!

When you feel weary, it's hard to have the heart for marketing. You haven't the impetus, the energy. You can't be bothered. It all seems false. And if your writing isn't going well, you can easily fall into the trap of not bothering to do any marketing, just sending out submissions with the briefest and dullest of covering letters. This is how you can change your state:

▶ Keep a skipping rope – skipping uses another side of your brain.

▶ Dance. The music needs to be loud and uplifting. Five minutes is enough.

▶ Tidy a small area of your room – a bookshelf or a tottering pile of magazines. Its neatness will uplift you.

▶ Walk or even jog round the block for five minutes, breathing deeply.

▶ Eat two squares of good organic chocolate – only two!

If you sometimes feel stressed (who doesn't?) and confused about your writing and marketing, here's some advice.

My students often tell me they just have so much in their mind – they can't corral it into an article. Or into a biography or a covering letter. They don't know where to start, or where to finish. To do a covering letter would be the last straw.

It's not their writing that's a problem – it's their emotions. I suffer from this sometimes. Beginning a brand new project is always hard for me – taking that first plunge onto a blank screen, or setting out my outline. Tapping out the first words. I'll think of ten ways to displace the activity – from getting a drink to cleaning the bath. The last thing I want to do is write. Like most of you, part of me thinks I'd rather spend the weekend relaxing or taking the train to Paris or shopping or having lunch with my friends. Other people are out having a good time. Why aren't we?

The trick is to re-frame it. It's not 'work' , but something that's a joy to do… something we want to do. Reward yourself with that trip, that lunch with friends, when and only when you've finished the project – when you've completed it and added the vital marketing pack – letter, picture and biography.

See your name in print

How's it going? Running out of steam? I know my advice can be relentless!

Here is my favourite visualisation to use again in the next ten minutes. It's a bit more powerful this time.

Take a break. Sit back on your sofa. Take all these stages slowly and keep them in your mind for at least several minutes – as long as you like. Think strong.

- ▶ Think strong, not weak
- ▶ See yourself buying a magazine
- ▶ Turn to the page with your article on
- ▶ Look at your own name and your picture there!
- ▶ Make the page big and bright
- ▶ Smile as you see your name and picture

You got there by writing, and by marketing yourself.

Come on, give yourself a pat on the back! If you can treat all your marketing projects with the care and the concentration you've allotted for this writing course weekend, you'll be amazed by how much you'll be able to achieve.

And you will achieve.

12 – Moving on

'Don't stop three feet from the gold. Go back and dig some more'

~ Henriette Anne Klauser, *Write It Down, Make It Happen*

You've completed your weekend writing course! You've succeeded in finishing a small body of work, and you've posted it off. Just one reader's letter or short opinion piece? You still deserve congratulations. The satisfaction is immense, isn't it? This is proof that you can create, polish and finish work. It's proof you are learning to coach yourself, and that you can achieve your goals. Let's build on this! What can you do to move your writing on in the next day, week, month and year? What can you do to keep going as a magazine writer?

One of the best things you can do is start to keep a writing diary, a daily record of thoughts, impressions, plans, and ideas – written honestly and carefully. Avoid the temptation to ramble. Aim for the kind of readability you'd find in a magazine feature, even when describing your own thoughts. When written like this, you will enjoy re-reading your diary much more.

You can write about people you've met, what you did, incidents you witnessed as you walked around your office, supermarket or town. Write down what happened at work – even the tension and arguments that are always there. Writing your way through stress is one of the best ways to beat it! You may even discover – as Ricky Gervais of *The Office* fame did – that workplace conflicts have their comic angles, and they're something to write about too.

I did this for three years, contributing regular personal columns, called Foibles, to *The Guardian*. I wrote about the ironies and comedies, the pleasures and miseries of office life. I used disguised (I hope) incidents from the very office I was working in, and though this never completely cured me of the occasional 'how-dare-he?' fury, it certainly helped!

141

How did I get this column? By following the suggestions in this book: sending in ideas and a sample; being honest in my writing; being unafraid to put a little piece of myself, frailties and all, on that page every week; and by being reliable – meeting every deadline, fitting their word-count (750) exactly, checking every fact and never writing anything that could be deemed offensive, although I often ridiculed office conventions, rules, rivalries and that strange language known as corporate-speak.

Look on your writing diary as a friend and confidante. Never let writing in it become a chore. When you don't have time or the inclination to write, don't beat yourself up – do it the next day. If you can manage just a few sentences...

> *Row with D at work. He shouted at me in front of my team, because I said I wanted the office music turned down. How dare he? He'll get his. I'm plotting my revenge even as I write. He'll be laughing on the other side of his face soon.*

... you might begin to see a glimmer of something that's very nearly like humour, and perhaps you're feeling better already? The memory of your row is becoming less oppressive. Writing to yourself can do this for you. I urge you to try it. Keeping my writing diary is essential for me. I couldn't be without it.

You can jot down your ideas for new articles in your lunch break, or when you're waiting to do the school pick-up, or when you have a blissful half-hour or so when the house is clean and tidy and nobody will be home until tea-time, or in the evening when the family's not there.

When you're out and about, take a note of new listings and facts and figures for your next magazine article. One of my very best places for writing is a pavement café in the sun, sipping a cappuccino. On holiday in a sunny European capital, free from routine and chores? Make sure your writing diary is in your luggage! You'll be inspired by the exotic setting, but don't expect to get all the writing done – that always comes later. For now, enjoy your break, let those impressions form and process them later.

Do it today!

What else can you do today – in the next 24 hours – to move your writing on?

Subscribe to writing magazines – they could be *Writers' News*, *Mslexia* (it's just for woman writers: www.mslexia.co.uk) or *Writers' Journal*. Look in Borders or WH Smith for a good selection of writing magazines, plus a magazine or two that you'd definitely like to write for – anything from *Wanderlust* to *She* or travel magazines about Italy or France. Promotional subscriptions can bring the cost down to as little as £1 a copy. You have the pleasure of the magazines dropping through your postbox, you'll build up a very good idea of what they want from writers – and if you buy by subscription you get gifts.

Here's another money-saver: ring up or go online to a bulk stationery company – they'll send you their catalogue. You'll find bulk products amazingly cheap. For example, fifty ballpoint pens will cost you about the same as twenty at retail prices. Envelopes, notebooks, folders, cartridges, copy paper – all are cheap and help you get that feeling of being an organized, professional writer. They have hundreds of stationery products. If you're a stationery junkie like me, you'll love them. Delivery is usually free. Try Office World at www.officeworld.com

On course

What can you do to move your writing on in a weekend or a week? You could take another course! These are six good weekend writing courses:

1   *Travel Writing*; runs one weekend, generally every month, Words and Pix. This two-day course is divided into useful sections for the budding travel writer; learn how to research, pitch, write, interview and use quotes. Includes practical exercises. £250.
    Tel 020 8692 4397, www.wordsandpix.co.uk

2   *Freelance Journalism for Beginners*; starts mid-October 2007, Bath University's Division for Life Long Learning, price to be announced. Workshops for novice writers looking to begin a career as a freelance journalist.
    Tel 01225 388704, www.bath.ac.uk/lifelong-learning

3   *Writing News and Features for Pleasure and Profit*; November 2007, Farncombe Estate Centre in the Cotswolds. An ideal taster course, for those who want to write news and features and learn the basic skills needed for magazine writers. Designed for both beginners and the more experienced. £55.
    Tel 0845 230 8590, www.farncombeestate.com

4   *How to market your work as a freelance journalist*; dates in March and May, 2007 at the City Lit, London. If you have ideas for features but are not sure how to get them into print or how to sell your ideas, this is the course for you. From £30.
    Tel 020 7492 2600, www.citylit.ac.uk

5   *News and feature writing*; generally every two months, NCTJ Training Ltd. Learn how to find ideas, write intros and endings and how to tighten up your writing. Other important areas are also covered. From £600.
    Tel 01799 544014, www.nctj.com

6 *Travel Writing and Photography*, 19 to 21 January 2007, Orlando, Florida. Annual course run by the Society of American Travel Writers, for writers and experienced travellers who want to improve their style. **www.satwinstitute.org**

Think about one of these one-week writing courses:

1 *A Writers Retreat to the Cotswolds*; April 2007, with Jane Blank. Farncombe Estate Centre. If you have a magazine project in mind and want to share your ideas or work in progress with a tutor and other writers, this is your chance to start or finish it! £180 excluding B&B. **Tel 0845 230 8590, www.farncombeestate.com**

2 *Travel Writing*; November 2007 at the Arvon Foundation's Totleigh Barton Centre, Devon. Learn about the art of travel writing, improve your skills and gain professional techniques at this well-established top writing centre. £475. **Tel 01409 231338, www.arvonfoundation.org**

3 *The Writer's Lab*; dates available from end of May until October 2007, Skyros Holidays. The Writer's Lab offers a number of first-class writing courses on Skyros Island in Greece, which are already attracting renowned writers. Guests can combine their writing with numerous other activities on offer, such as yoga, dance, watersports, music. Inspiring, healthy and you'll come home with new friends and a tan! **Tel 020 7267 4424, www.skyros.co.uk**

4 *Write Articles that Sell*; courses in Malaga planned for May, June, September and October 2007 (special weeks for groups can be arranged at other times) with Stella Whitelaw. Workshops take place in the morning, while guests can choose how to spend their afternoons – continuing writing or sightseeing. Evening talks about writing and publishing. Excellent tuition in a beautiful setting. **Tel 01454-773579, www.malagaworkshops.co.uk**

5 *Travel, food and wine writing*; June 10-15, 2007 in St. Emilion, France. The Writer's Workshop's luxury five-day course introduces guests to the skills needed for travel, food and wine writing. Includes visits to wineries and historic sights. Approximately £1,300. **Tel 001 206 284 7121, www.thewritersworkshop.net**

6 Wellbeing Holidays *Go After What You Want* workshops on Iraklia island, Greece. A week's course in your own luxury studio. Pam Rigden's gentle but effective coaching with NLP will move your goals on – you get the workshop plus three hours one to one with her. Not a writing course, but a coaching week that will enhance your confidence and wellbeing. From £450. **www.wellbeing-holidays.co.uk: relax@wellbeing-holidays.co.uk**

Commit to a year

Thinking of taking your writing skills even further? There are many inspiring 12-month writing courses. You'll get plenty of opportunities to meet magazine writers, editors and agents. As a student on one of these courses, you're in a privileged position to fast-track your writing. You may not even have to go in every day, as some work is done from your own home, and there are long holidays. I'd look on these courses as an investment, maybe a luxury; you might be doing one as a mature student, using money from an insurance or redundancy package. I've seen the programmes for these courses and they're pretty impressive.

1   Professional Writing MA/Postgraduate Dip; University College, Falmouth, October 2007. This course teaches the core skills needed for writing for different markets as well as how to become pro-active in selling your work. Students will specialize in at least two different areas of writing – one of which could be writing for magazines. £3,120.

    Tel 01326 211077, www.falmouth.ac.uk

2   MA Creative Writing; Bath Spa University, October 2007. This highly-regarded course in creative writing is taught by writers, such as novelists Mimi Thebo and Mo Hayder. Many modules on offer, including reviewing, article writing and journalism. £3,480.

    Tel 01225 875875, www.bathspa.ac.uk

3   MA/Postgraduate Dip Magazine Journalism; Bournemouth University, September 2007. This new course aims to equip students with all of the necessary skills needed to write for a range of publications as well as understanding the law and ethics involved in writing for magazines. £4,800.

    Tel 01202 965371, www.bournemouth.ac.uk

4   MA/Postgraduate Diploma Journalism; London College of Communication, September 2007. This intensive course allows students to specialize in a range of areas and to benefit from a work placement during the course. Modules include magazine article, feature and news writing, reporting, interviewing and page layout. £3,218.

    Tel 020 7514 6800, www.lcc.arts.ac.uk

5   Postgraduate Diploma Magazine Journalism; Cardiff University, October 2007. Students are taught how to write news and features, how to market their own work, plus sub-editing and shorthand skills. You will also create your own magazine as part of an assignment. £5,095.

    Tel 029 2087 4000, www.cardiff.ac.uk

One-day writer?

With a full-time or in a part-time job, you might have only one day a week free. That's still quite a lot! These are time management and coaching tips if you have only one day or afternoon a week to spare for writing.

▶ TRY to get basic chores done in advance. Order groceries online for delivery on Thursday and Friday and – if you can possibly manage it – a cleaner for two hours on Friday will kick-start your weekend. Shining floors and piles of ironing done by someone else will free you up, physically and mentally, to write. Or, pay a family member or a student to be your cleaner for an hour.

▶ MAKE a list of writing goals that can be achieved in the day or afternoon; give yourself the task of finishing just one short article, or two reader's letters each day you set aside for your writing.

▶ KEEP everything in separate folders. With just one day a week to work in, you don't want to waste it searching for bits of paper. Buy plenty of folders.

▶ HAVE a space that is just for your writing; a small room or desk with filing space.

▶ YOUR writing time is precious. Seeing someone for lunch or cramming in errands will eat into it and sap your concentration. Try to reserve the entire day if you can.

▶ HAVE dinner a bit later than usual and have easy foods ready – or see if your partner will cook for you!

▶ WORK on your writing during the week, on the train or bus on your way to work.

▶ PERHAPS you don't even have as much as a day? If you have just one evening, make notes for one article and keep working on that until it's finished. Give yourself a limit of five evening sessions in which to have it finished and sent out.

Fit to write

You need to stay fit to write – and writing can be a very unhealthy occupation! These are some typical questions put to my favourite GP, Dr Milind Jani (Email: dr.jani@pavilionhealth.co.uk www.pavilionhealth.co.uk). Based in Brighton, he specializes in gentle yet effective holistic therapies and has his own range of products, many of them made from Indian herbs and flowers.

Q *My problem is having too many ideas for magazine articles – I do not know which one to start on first. Consequently, I often end up feeling drained and exhausted, yet have accomplished no writing. Can you advise?*

A Regular meditation is the best way to focus your mind. One way to decide which idea to develop is to think about your ideas while doing meditation. The idea which calls your attention again and again is the one you fancy! Think of your teenage years when you had five great looking girlfriends or boyfriends. The one who drew your attention again and again was the one you wanted to be with. Writing is like a passionate love affair!

Q *After a day at the computer, my back is aching. I am 34, quite fit, work from home and have not got a proper office chair, so I put a lot of cushions on an ordinary chair for now. Have you any tips on reducing strain?*

A Most back strains for sedentary workers are from stiffness due to prolonged lack of movement and poor posture-slouching of back and neck at the desk. You should invest in a proper chair with good low back support. Avoid chairs with high backs. Get up every half-hour and stretch your back. Have you done any yoga? Try to sign up to a yoga class! A drop-in class doesn't commit you to paying a large sum ahead, and you will find your body becomes more flexible and your concentration for writing improves. Massage your back with your fists to release the knotting. Thump your back with the back of your fists. Regular massage with RheumaEase oil – mahanarayan oil from Pavilion Healthcare – on neck and back will help prevent chronic back stiffness and pain.

Q *I want to write magazine articles and have two days a week to work on them; the rest of the week I am an office administrator. I start off well, but often seem to run out of energy in the afternoon and can't get inspired. Any health tricks to keep me writing?*

A Do regular yogic breathing to provide oxygen and nutrition to the brain cells. Drink Ginger pick-me-up tea or Stress-Aid tea (Pavilion Health-care) two or three times a day particularly in the afternoon to stimulate you and revive energy. Spices such as ginger, black pepper and nutmeg in a balanced proportion help to boost your writing energy.

Q *I'm at my desk writing all day at work – constantly snacking on chocolate bars and crisps. Then I write magazine articles at home and do the same, stocking up with multi-packs of crisps and peanut bars – my major downfall! Consequently I am putting on weight. Can you recommend energy-boosting foods which will be interesting to eat when I write – but healthier?*

A Sesame seed flapjack with molasses is a very healthy nourishing snack which gives more sustained energy, along with vitamin E, calcium and iron. Or eat a sandwich with brown bread, salad, tomato and mango chutney. This will fill you up in a healthy way.

Q *When I get a rejection slip I feel depressed all day. It takes me a day at least to get over it! My friends who write magazine articles say the same. Is there a way to stop this feeling of being undermined?*

A Despondency after rejection is directly related to self-esteem and the demands we make on ourselves and the world. According to Rational Emotive Behaviour Therapy (REBT), it is the 'should' and 'must' – for example, the "I must not be rejected ever" response that creates an irrational demand that feeds despondency. Change the false belief system of demand to a preference: "I would much prefer not to be rejected, but I can take it if I am, because there is no guarantee in life." Use self-reaffirmation more often and consciously: "I tried my best, being rejected does not mean I am no good, only that my writing style did not match their expectation this time." Have a long-term view: there's plenty of life ahead, with new opportunities. Enjoy and celebrate the process of writing, not just the outcome. Remind yourself of your other achievements.

Q *My job is stressful, working in copywriting, writing press and promotional copy about central heating for demanding and unimaginative bosses. I really want to be a writer for women's magazines and I work at that some evenings. But the stress of the day job means I often wake around 4a.m. and sleep badly. I don't have other problems, just the job really. If I could sleep better, I could cope better, but I don't want to take pills. I have not found herbal tablets with valerian much good. Can you suggest other remedies?*

A Stress management requires personal discipline at balancing one's energies. The secret of good sleep lies in balancing different activities. Some exercise during the day will tire you and promote good sleep. Some meditation with relaxing music and deep breathing in the evening will help. Drink a glass of warm milk with my almonds and nutmeg sleep-promoting recipe (Peaceful Sleep mixture from Pavilion Health).

6 ways to keep going!

You can keep up your magazine writing energy by:

1   Staying disciplined – remember my mantra: finish your articles and send them out!

2   Writing down your goals on Friday night for each weekend. You may not want to work through the entire weekend, but maybe you could set aside two hours for your writing?

3   Keeping your writing space neat and tidy.

4   Saving news snippets and articles which could be useful. Don't save the whole magazine or journal, just cut out the piece you need. Don't forget to date it and make a note of the publication.   *file it in folder*

5   Looking in WH Smith and other shops for new magazine markets – magazines you would like to write for. Also look in magazines such as Writers' News which report on all the new magazine markets and what they want. Often a new magazine will send out an initial copy free, and they may have writers guidelines you can send for.

6   Keeping up with new products in stationery shops. The smallest item might be of use and could even inspire you. Coloured paperclips, postcard-size coloured plastic folders, commemorative stamps have all inspired me and made my writing day a little lighter.

Best books for magazine writers

▶   *Writing for Magazines: A Beginner's Guide*, £23.99, Cheryl Wray, McGraw-Hill Education, tel 01628 502720, www.mcgraw-hill.co.uk – A comprehensive guide to all you need to know about this demanding market. Includes tips on writing style, basic rules of grammar and helpful exercises.

▶   *Writing Short Stories and Articles: How to Get Your Work Published in Newspapers and Magazines*, £8.99, Adele Ramet, How To Books, tel 01865 375794, www.howtobooks.co.uk. It focuses on all of the important elements of writing for print: how to construct an article, how to adapt your style for different audiences and how to market your work. It also has a useful section on how to become a freelance writer.

▶ *Travel Writing*, £10.99, Don George. Lonely Planet Publications, tel 020 7841 9000, www.lonelyplanet.com – Learn how to turn your tales into brilliant, publishable travel features with the aid of this inspiring book. Includes interviews with writers, editors and agents.

▶ *Writing Feature Articles*, £21.99, Brendan Hennessy, Focal Press, tel 01865 474010, www.focalpress.com – Find out how to write great articles and exploit the market with this all-encompassing guide. It has a section on writing for online publications, making it up-to-speed with the changing face of the media.

▶ *Writing for Journalists*, £12.99, Wynford Hicks, ISBN: 0415184452, Routledge, tel 020 7017 6000, www.routledge.com – Discover how to capture the readers' attention and make them want to carry on reading; includes a glossary of journalistic jargon.

Writing magazines

▶ *Mslexia*: For women who write; Quarterly, (available in Borders or on subscription), £5.50, Mslexia Publications Ltd, 0191 261 6656; www.mslexia.co.uk – The most prestigious magazine for women writers, covering everything from writers' block to travel writing. Contemporary, relevant and inspiring, it includes listings of competitions and regional events.

▶ *Writing Magazine*; monthly, £3.40, published by Writers' News Ltd, tel 0113 200 2929, www.writingmagazine.co.uk. A practical, industry-focused magazine, with a team of columnists – from journalists to published authors – offering tips on writing as well as inspiring ideas for the readers' own work.

▶ *Writers' News*; monthly, £3.50, published by Writers' News Ltd, tel 0113 200 2929, www.writersnews.co.uk. Everything you need to know about the writing world; all the latest market information and advice, with great tips on what editors are looking for. The writers 'bible'.

▶ *Writers' Forum*; monthly, £3.50, tel 01202 589828, www.writers-forum.com. A magazine dedicated to writers working in all genres – fiction, scriptwriting, poetry and magazines. It includes competitions and inspiring articles.

▶ *Writers' Journal*; bi-monthly, £4.95, (available in Borders or on subscription), tel 001 218-346-7921, www.writersjournal.com – An American magazine covering almost every angle of writing that you could possibly think of, including how to write for magazines. Why not enter its annual travel writing contest?

Relaxing and motivating CD's – ideal for magazine writers

▶ *The Power To Change*, £13.95, Ian McDermott, International Teaching Seminars, tel 01268 777125 www.itsnlp.com Allow Ian's amazingly relaxing voice to enhance your motivation, and harness your enthusiasm to meet your goals. Includes a "hit list" of essential tips. Inspiring, soothing, effective. In my view, he's the best.

▶ *Learn How To Think Positively*, £11.95, Glenn Harrold, Diviniti Publishing, tel 01732 220373, www.hypnosisaudio.com. Teaches you how to develop a more positive outlook on life, feel more confident and create a more satisfying future.

▶ *Instant Confidence* (free – as part of the book) £9.99 Paul McKenna Bantam Press. The CD is part of Paul's book, *Instant Confidence*, which aims to give you 'the power to go for anything you want'. Learn how to master your emotions and fill your mind with positive thoughts and feelings. Programme your mind for success in your writing.

▶ *Energy & Motivation*, £11.95, Glenn Harrold, Diviniti Publishing, tel 01732 220373, www.hypnosisaudio.com. Designed to give the listener energy, inspiration and motivation; you should be writing magazine articles almost straight after listening to it!

▶ *An introduction to NLP: Psychological Skills For Understanding and Influencing People*, £13.99, Joseph O'Connor and Ian McDermott, Harper Thorsons Element, tel 0870 900 2050, www.thorsonselement. com. A beginner's guide to this popular development in applied psychology. Neuro-Linguistic Programming has been very effective in changing people's attitudes and building up confidence. If falling out with people at work has dented your writing energy, this is the one to try. My coach uses NLP and I've been following his advice for years with success.

Useful websites – yes, there are some!

▶ www.nuj.org.uk – National Union of Journalists: The country's largest trade union for journos – magazines, newspapers and other media – has a website packed with information for aspiring and working journalists.

▶ www.swwj.co.uk – Society of Women Writers and Journalists: Promoting professional standards, literary achievement and contact with fellow women writers, editors, magazine writers, publishers, broadcasters and agents.

▶ www.journobiz.com – JournoBiz.com: Join this online community for journalists. Members can share information and get discounts and many other benefits.

- ▶ www.nctj.com – The National Council for the Training of Journalists (NCTJ): Find a suitable magazine journalism course or training scheme – all of the courses listed are accredited by the council.

- ▶ www.writersbureau.com – The Writers Bureau: Offers home-study courses in freelance journalism, article writing plus much more, along with other resources such as the highly-useful Freelance Market News.

You say goodbye, I say hello

That's it. We've finished, for now!

I want to thank you for taking my course. It's been a privilege to have you as a student. But the rest depends on you. Try to keep going even when you don't feel like writing. When you think it's just too hard to finish something and send it off, that's the time to re-read bits of this book and redouble your efforts. And you will!

But don't let's say goodbye. From one magazine writer to another, let's say hello! You can e-mail me at my writing club at diana@canalstreet.org.uk

Southampton Solent University

Why not join one of our exciting and innovative journalism degrees?

We have a well established record of journalism training and are currently recruiting for:

BA (Hons) Magazine Journalism and Feature Writing
BA (Hons) Writing Fashion and Culture
BA (Hons) Journalism (Print and Broadcast Pathways)
BA (Hons) On-Line Journalism
BA (Hons) Sports Writing

All our students are trained in both practical journalism production and cultural theory, and our highly acclaimed BA (Hons) Journalism degree is accredited by the NCTJ, BJTC and PTC.

Southampton Solent University
East Park Terrace
Southampton
Hampshire
SO14 0YN
Tel: +44 (0) 23 8031 9000
www.solent.ac.uk

Southampton
SOLENT
University

LORETTA PROCTOR has been writing since her early teens. An Anglo-Greek born in Egypt, she came to England as a small child, living in London for many years. She now lives in Malvern, UK, with her husband, John, and has two children who live in London. This is her brand new novel.

THE LONG SHADOW OF MACEDONIAN GREECE CAUGHT IN A DEVASTATING WORLD WAR...

Fourteen-year-old Andrew discovers his mother's hidden diary at his grandmother's home during a Christmas gathering. His eyes are opened to a family secret when he reads about her time as a nurse in Salonika during the First World War, and the tragic love affair she had with his father, a Greek Officer who died in battle. Four years later, Andrew is impelled to visit his father's land and trace his roots. What – and who – he finds there will change his life forever.

The Long Shadow is filled with description of Greece and its people. Dramatic images of battle and the terrible conditions endured by Allied Armies entrenched around Salonika in the "Birdcage" are authentic and vivid. Greek music and dance play a vital role, reconciling in Andrew the dichotomy of belonging to two very different cultures and helping him to unite them in his heart and soul.

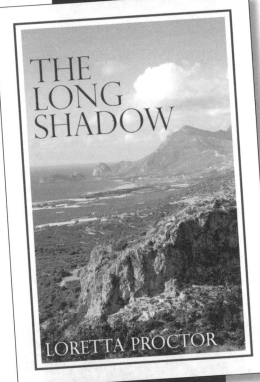

...A SHADOW THAT FELL OVER MANY LIVES... CHANGING THEM FOREVER

Publish America ISBN 1-4241-0109-3 price £14.95 (also available online with Amazon, Borders, Gardners, Ingrams) Goldsboro Books, I Cecil Court, WC2 and Murder One, 73 Charing Cross Rd. WC2 have copies instore.

PUBLISH AMERICA

www.PublishAmerica.com

Malaga**Workshops**

Enjoy a relaxing and effective writing or photography course in the UK or in Spain

Malaga Workshops are highly recommended by new and experienced writers for their careful, professional and friendly tuition and the beautiful settings they are held in. Course leader Geraldine O'Neill runs a "**Develop Your Novel**" writing weekend at Burton Manor, Cheshire, from 10 to 12 November 2006 and 16 to 18 February 2007.

She offers an exclusive holiday course in Andalucia, Spain on "**The Novel**" from 1 to 8 October 2006. Course leader John Townsend presents a weekend course "**Write for Children**" at Burton Manor, Cheshire, 13 to 15 October 2006. Photography courses for beginners and improvers are held in spectacular Grazalema Natural Park, Spain. Places are booked up swiftly, so early booking is recommended. For more details on courses and dates, tel 00 44 (0) 1454 773579, e-mail root@malagaworkshops,co.uk or visit www.malagaworkshops.co.uk

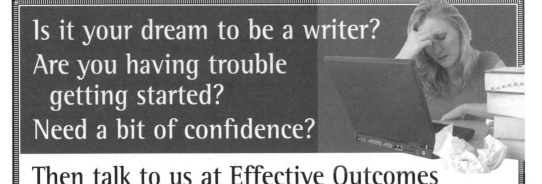

HighGrove Estate

by E. George Perrott

This is the story of Tony, 23 years old, and his love affair
with Linda, a divorcee, 14 years his senior.

A blighted situation surrounding these two people and their families
where jealousy from an earlier affair creates a set of circumstances
which almost wrecks Tony's life.

The background of the book is set in the late 1970s
and early 1980s during Mrs Thatcher's
reign as Prime Minister.

£7.99

Gemini Publications

ISBN 0-9530637-8-X

Diana Cambridge, author of *How to
write for magazines ...in one weekend*
gave George Perrott extensive assistance
in the structure of this novel.

Win Lonely Planet books and see your work published!

Like to see your travel feature published in a book? Enter our Travel Writing contest – the winning entry will be printed in Diana Cambridge's next book, *How To Write Travel Articles... In One Weekend* (Canal Street Publishing Ltd, £12.99).

When you plan your next holiday, why not take the advice in this book and turn your travel experiences into an article? Or you can write a travel feature based on your own town or city or neighbourhood.

We'd love you to enter our Canal Street Travel Writing contest. There's £100 worth of Lonely Planet books – including Don George's excellent *Lonely Planet Guide to Travel Writing* (£10.99) – waiting for the winner. Lonely Planet have been leaders in producing exemplary guidebooks for independent travellers since the 1970s. There are now more than 500 great books in their second-to-none range. Don's book is an inspirational and practical guide – he's a renowned travel writer and editor and has been teaching travel writing for 15 years. Find out more at www.lonelyplanet.com

Our judge will be travel magazine editor David Kernek, who edits both the international *Holiday Villas* magazine and *Holiday Cottages* magazine, which focuses on vacations in the UK and Ireland. He is a former award-winning editor of *The Northern Echo*, and a Fellow of the prestigious World Press Institute in Minneapolis/St Paul. As a young journalist, David won a year's travel in the States. This is one of his key tips for new travel writers:

> *A strong lead in – the opening paragraphs – is essential, because that is what is going to make an editor carry on reading the feature. It could be a dramatic description, a humorous anecdote or a snatch of a conversation. Whatever it is, it has to be compelling – something that stops the reader putting the magazine down and turning on the television instead.*

- **Your feature should be no more than 1,200 words, typed or word-processed on one side of the paper only.**

- **Attach a label which includes:**
  Your name and address
  Day-time phone number
  Email address
  Title of your article
  A few lines about you (400 words max.)

- **Don't forget to keep a copy – entries are non-returnable.**

Your entry needs to be posted to us (sorry – no entries by email) by May 15, 2007 and the winning entry will be published in *How To Write Travel Articles... In One Weekend* by Diana Cambridge (Canal Street Publishing Ltd, £12.99 2007). Five runners-up names will also be published. Each of the five will win a copy of *Mountains of Europe* (Alistair Sawday £9.99) – a travel guide to Europe's special ski hotels, restaurants and places to stay. You'll find the writing in the Alistair Sawday travel guides is the best, cliché-free and refreshing – visit the website www.specialplacestostay.com to find out more.

Entries should be sent to:

Travel Writing Competition 2007,
Canal Street Publishing Ltd,
1 Coburg Villas,
Camden Road,
Bath, Somerset, BA1 5JF.

All entries are non-returnable.
There is no cash alternative to the prizes.
Winners will be informed by June 30, 2007.